The following study guides by Dawn Apgar are also available to assist social workers with studying for and passing the ASWB® examinations.

Bachelors

The Social Work ASWB® Bachelors Exam Guide: A Comprehensive Guide for Success, Second Edition

Test focuses on knowledge acquired while obtaining a Baccalaureate degree in Social Work (BSW). A small number of jurisdictions license social workers at an Associate level and require the ASWB Associate examination. The Associate examination is identical to the ASWB Bachelors examination, but the Associate examination requires a lower score in order to pass.

Masters

The Social Work ASWB® Masters Exam Guide: A Comprehensive Guide for Success, Second Edition

Test focuses on knowledge acquired while obtaining a Master's degree in Social Work (MSW). There is no postgraduate supervision needed.

Clinical

The Social Work ASWB® Clinical Exam Guide: A Comprehensive Guide for Success, Second Edition

Test focuses on knowledge acquired while obtaining a Master's degree in Social Work (MSW). It is usually taken by those with postgraduate supervised experience.

Advanced Generalist

The Social Work ASWB® Advanced Generalist Exam Guide: A Comprehensive Guide for Success, Second Edition

Test focuses on knowledge acquired while obtaining a Master's degree in Social Work (MSW). It is usually taken by those with postgraduate supervised nonclinical experience.

Dawn Apgar, PhD, LSW, ACSW, has helped thousands of social workers across the country pass the ASWB® examinations associated with all levels of licensure. In recent years, she has consulted in numerous states to assist with establishing licensure test preparation programs.

Dr. Apgar has done research on licensure funded by the American Foundation for Research and Consumer Education in Social Work Regulation and has served as chairperson of her state's social work licensing board. She is a past President of the New Jersey Chapter of NASW and has been on its National Board of Directors. In 2014, the Chapter presented her with a Lifetime Achievement Award. Dr. Apgar has taught in both undergraduate and graduate social work programs and has extensive direct practice, policy, and management experience in the social work field.

Social Work ASWB® Bachelors Practice Test

170 Questions to Identify Knowledge Gaps

Second Edition

Dawn Apgar, PhD, LSW, ACSW

SPRINGER PUBLISHING COMPANY

Copyright © 2018 Springer Publishing Company, LLC

All rights reserved.

No part of this publication may be reproduced, stored in a retrieval system, or transmitted in any form or by any means, electronic, mechanical, photocopying, recording, or otherwise, without the prior permission of Springer Publishing Company, LLC, or authorization through payment of the appropriate fees to the Copyright Clearance Center, Inc., 222 Rosewood Drive, Danvers, MA 01923, 978-750-8400, fax 978-646-8600, info@copyright.com or on the Web at www.copyright.com.

Springer Publishing Company, LLC
11 West 42nd Street
New York, NY 10036
www.springerpub.com

Acquisitions Editor: Debra Riegert
Compositor: diacriTech

ISBN: 978-0-8261-4724-0
ebook ISBN: 978-0-8261-4725-7

17 18 19 20 21 / 5 4 3 2 1

The author and the publisher of this Work have made every effort to use sources believed to be reliable to provide information that is accurate and compatible with the standards generally accepted at the time of publication. The author and publisher shall not be liable for any special, consequential, or exemplary damages resulting, in whole or in part, from the readers' use of, or reliance on, the information contained in this book. The publisher has no responsibility for the persistence or accuracy of URLs for external or third-party Internet websites referred to in this publication and does not guarantee that any content on such websites is, or will remain, accurate or appropriate.

Library of Congress Cataloging-in-Publication Data
Names: Apgar, Dawn, author. | Association of Social Work Boards.
Title: Social work ASWB bachelors practice test : 170 questions to identify
    knowledge gaps / Dawn Apgar, PhD, LSW, ACSW.
Description: Second edition. | New York, NY : Springer Publishing Company, LLC, [2018]
Identifiers: LCCN 2017044815 | ISBN 9780826147240 | ISBN 9780826147257 (ebook)
Subjects: LCSH: Social workers—Certification—United States. | Social
    service—United States—Examinations—Study guides. | Social
    service—United States—Examinations, questions, etc.
Classification: LCC HV40.52 .A7354 2018 | DDC 361.3076—dc23 LC record available at
https://lccn.loc.gov/2017044815

Contact us to receive discount rates on bulk purchases.
We can also customize our books to meet your needs.
For more information please contact: sales@springerpub.com

Printed in the United States of America by Gasch Printing.

To Bill, Ryan, and Alex

You remind me what is important, support me so I can do it all, and always inspire me to be a better person

Contents

Contents

Introduction

Despite social workers' best efforts to study for and pass the Association of Social Work Boards (ASWB®) examinations for licensure, they can encounter difficulties answering questions correctly that can ultimately lead to challenges in passing. Social workers who struggle with standardized test taking or have failed the ASWB examinations find themselves at a loss in finding resources to assist them in identifying the mistakes they made and strategies for correcting those errors. The focus of test preparation courses and guides is usually the review of the relevant content and supplying some study and test-taking tips. However, when these resources do not result in passing the ASWB examinations, social workers do not know where to turn for help.

Often, social workers will turn to taking practice tests in an effort to gauge their readiness for the ASWB examinations. In addition, they will try to use them to identify gaps in knowledge and errors in problem solving that prevent desired outcomes. Such an approach is understandable because there has been a void in available diagnostic resources. However, for several reasons, use of existing practice examinations is not usually helpful.

First, it is difficult to identify specific content that is used by test developers to formulate actual questions. For example, many practice tests do not provide the rationales for the correct and incorrect answers. In addition, they usually do not let social workers know which specific ASWB® content areas were being tested (e.g., Human Development, Diversity, and Behavior in the Environment; Assessment; Interventions With Clients/Client Systems; or Professional Relationships, Values, and Ethics). In addition, the ASWB competencies and corresponding Knowledge, Skills, and

Abilities statements (KSAs) that form the basis for question development are also not included. Thus, when questions are answered incorrectly, social workers do not know which knowledge in the ASWB content areas, competencies, and KSAs is lacking so they can go back and review relevant source materials.

Based on a practice analysis conducted by ASWB, which outlines the content to be included on the exam, content areas, competencies, and KSAs are created. Content areas are the broad knowledge areas that are measured by each exam. The content areas structure the content for exam construction and score reporting purposes. When receiving exam scores, failing candidates are given feedback on their performance on each content area of the exam. Competencies describe meaningful *sets* of abilities that are important to the job of a social worker within each content area. Finally, KSAs structure the content of the exam for item development purposes. The KSAs provide further details about the nature and range of exam content that is included in the competencies. Each KSA describes a discrete knowledge component that is the basis for individual exam questions that may be used to measure the competency.

Having ASWB content areas, competencies, and KSAs identified is critical in order to make practice tests useful for diagnosing knowledge weaknesses. The following example illustrates the usefulness of having this material explicitly stated.

SAMPLE QUESTION

A social worker at a community mental health agency is doing a home visit to a client as he has not gotten his medication refilled as prescribed. The social worker learns that he has not been taking it for several weeks due to a belief that it is not helping to alleviate his thought to "just end things." In order to assist the client, the social worker should FIRST:

  A. Accompany the client to his next appointment with the psychiatrist to see if another medication can be prescribed
  B. Explain to the client the importance of taking the medication as prescribed
  C. Conduct a suicide risk assessment
  D. Ask the client if he has suggestions for other strategies that may assist him

ANSWER

1. C

Rationale

Social workers have an ethical duty to respect and promote the right of clients to self-determination. However, there are times when **social workers' responsibility to the larger society** or specific legal obligations supersedes their commitment to respecting clients' decisions or wishes. These instances are when, *in the social workers' professional judgment*, clients' actions or potential actions pose a serious, foreseeable, and imminent risk to themselves (including the risk of suicide) or others (in general or aimed at identifiable third parties—duty to warn).

The client's thoughts to "just end things" may be an indicator of suicide risk. The social worker should FIRST assess the degree of risk which is present to determine whether the client is safe without use of the medication and can wait to discuss his concerns with his psychiatrist at a future appointment or needs to be treated immediately, voluntarily, or involuntarily.

Knowledge Area

Unit III—Interventions With Clients/Client Systems (Content Area); Indicators and Effects of Crisis and Change (Competency); The Indicators and Risk Factors of the Client's/Client System's Danger to Self and Others (KSA)

If this answer was missed, social workers need the rationale for the correct response choice in order to identify the need to review materials related to interventions with clients/client systems, which is the content area being assessed. Specifically, this question focused on determining competency with regard to identifyng indicators of client danger to self or others (KSA). Reviewing the risk factors and signs associated with suicide would be a useful place to start. In addition, refined literature searches on self-determination and dignity of risk would produce more targeted information to fill this information gap.

Most practice tests will not help direct social workers toward these resources as they do not provide the ASWB content areas, competencies, and KSAs being tested. They also do not give valuable information on the topics as a way for social workers to understand the rationales for the correct answers and why the others are incorrect.

Second, practice tests rarely explicitly identify the test-taking strategies that must be used in order to select the correct answers from the others provided. Even when rationales are provided on practice tests, the test-taking strategies that should be generalized to other questions are often not explicitly stated. This void makes it difficult for social workers to see problems that they may be having in problem solving, outside of content gaps.

For example, in the sample question, social workers must be keenly aware of the client's thoughts to "just end things" as delineated by quotation marks. These thoughts may be an indication of suicide risk.

There is also a qualifying word—FIRST—used, which is capitalized in the question. The use of this qualifying word indicates that more than one of the provided response choices may be correct, but selecting the one that precedes the others is what is being asked. When clients are potentially suicidal, social workers must FIRST assess for risk.

This tool was developed to assist social workers in identifying their knowledge gaps and difficulties in problem solving by providing critical information including the knowledge area being assessed and the test-taking strategies required in order to answer questions correctly.

Social workers should use this diagnostic practice test to identify:

- Question wording that is important to selecting correct answers
- Key social work concepts that are being assessed
- Useful problem-solving strategies and themes
- Mistakes in logic
- Content areas, competencies, and/or KSAs that require additional study

This test is not intended to be a study guide, but it does contain important social work content related to the KSAs. This diagnostic practice test helps social workers who are struggling to find answers about what mistakes they are making and what they need to study more. It can be used in conjunction with existing study guides that provide an overview of needed social work material, such as the *Social Work ASWB® Bachelors Exam Guide: A Comprehensive Guide for Success, Second Edition* by this author.

Social workers must understand their learning styles and use available resources to fill in existing content gaps through the use of visual, auditory, and/or hands-on materials. Most social work content is available for little or no cost. There is no need to purchase expensive products as there are many educational materials available for free. However, it is important that social workers make sure that these resources are rooted in the values and knowledge base of the profession, as well as produced by those providing legitimate instruction. There are no tricks or fast facts for the examination that can replace learning and understanding a topic. The application of material requires being able to relate it to various case scenarios or vignettes.

Recommendations for Using This Practice Test

Actual ASWB test results are based on 150 scored items and an additional 20 questions that are not scored because they are being piloted. These pilot items are intermixed with the scored ones and not distinguished in any way. Social workers never find out which questions are scored and which questions are being piloted.

In an effort to make this diagnosis as similar to the examination as possible, it contains 170 questions, the same number as the actual exam, proportionately distributed within the four domains—Human Development, Diversity, and Behavior in the Environment (43 questions); Assessment (49 questions); Interventions With Clients/Client Systems (44 questions); and Professional Relationships, Values, and Ethics (34 questions). These proportions mirror the distribution of questions across these domains on the actual ASWB® examination.

The best way for social workers to use this practice test is to:

- Complete it after you have studied yet are still feeling uncertain about problem areas
- Finish it completely during a 4-hour block of time as a way of gauging fatigue and the length of time it will take to complete the actual examination
- Avoid looking up the answers until you have finished completely

- Generate a list of content areas in which you experienced problems and use it as the basis of a study plan employing other source materials to further review the concepts
- Generalize the test-taking strategies for future use on the actual examination

This practice test is to be used as a diagnostic tool, so social workers should not worry about getting incorrect answers, but should view them as learning opportunities to avoid common pitfalls and pinpoint learning needs. On the actual ASWB examination, the number of questions that social workers need to answer correctly generally varies from 93 to 106 of the 150 scored items. Since this diagnostic practice test contains 170 items, 20 questions would need to be randomly removed (6 from Unit I, 5 from Unit II, 5 from Unit III, and 4 from Unit IV) to determine if the overall number correct falls into this range.[1] Since many social workers who do not pass find themselves "just missing" these pass points, the value of identifying content gaps and difficulties in problem solving is tremendous because it can result in additional correct answers on the actual test.

---

[1]   Because different test takers receive different questions, raw scores on the actual exam—the actual number of correctly answered questions—go through an "equating process" to make sure that those receiving more difficult questions are not placed at a disadvantage. Equating adjusts the number of items needed to be answered correctly up or down depending on the difficulty levels. This diagnostic practice test has not gone through the equating process, which is why the number of correct answers needed to "pass" using ASWB standards cannot be determined.

170-Question Diagnostic Practice Test

1. A client who has recently retired tells a social worker that his life has always been consumed by his job. He was focused on rising to the top of his industry and increasing his earnings. The client feels that he would now like to "make a difference by giving back" and would like to donate his time and money to helping others. This client is MOST likely:

   A. Progressing through a typical psychosocial stage of development
   B. Worrying about having something productive to do now that he is retired
   C. Wanting to teach others how to be successful in their chosen fields
   D. Experiencing a loss in role functioning that often accompanies retirement

2. A social worker is asked to evaluate the effectiveness of a behavioral program aimed at increasing social skills of children. While collecting baseline data, she asks a colleague to independently record the number of social interactions observed prior to the start of the program. The colleague's information is then compared to that obtained by the social worker. This approach is MOST likely used by the social worker due to concerns about:

   A. Validity of the research being conducted
   B. Response bias due to social desirability
   C. Reliability of the observations made
   D. Homogeneity of the sample

3. Which of the following is NOT an assumption of age-stage developmental theorists?

   A. Development is discontinuous, with qualitatively different capacities emerging in each stage.
   B. Stages are related to age.
   C. Stages occur in a specific order, with each stage building on capacities developed in the previous stage.
   D. Development in early childhood has an impact on development later in life.

4. A process during which a conditioned response gradually stops occurring due to the withholding of a reinforcer is known as:

   A. Aversion therapy
   B. Negative reinforcement
   C. Extinction
   D. Classical conditioning

5. Which of the following service provisions is based on a residual approach to social welfare?

   A. Public education
   B. Supplemental nutrition assistance
   C. Law enforcement
   D. Social Security

6. A client reports getting fired from her job. When asked about the reason for her termination, she states that it was due to her boss being jealous of her. However, performance appraisals reveal that the client was late for work and did not complete tasks accurately or in a timely fashion. The client is MOST likely using which of the following defense mechanisms with regard to her firing?

   A. Rationalization
   B. Displacement
   C. Projection
   D. Conversion

7. Which of the following statements is true about BOTH consultants and supervisors in social work?

   A. Consultants have specialized expertise while supervisors are generalists.
   B. Consultants and supervisors provide time-limited assistance in solving identified problems.

C. Consultants charge high fees for their services while supervisors do not.

D. Consultants have no formal authority within organizations while supervisors do.

8. Which of the following is NOT a purpose of licensing social work practice?

A. To establish regulations to serve as standards for professional practice

B. To provide a mechanism for gatekeeping of those who do not have requisite knowledge and/or education from practicing

C. To raise social work salaries so that they are more closely aligned with other licensed professionals

D. To monitor those in practice to ensure compliance with established rules, taking remedial action as needed

9. The primary focus of crisis intervention in social work is to:

A. Help clients learn coping skills so that they can avoid the onset of crises in the future

B. Provide immediate assistance to address presenting problems

C. Identify factors that have caused the crises for the development of preventative measures

D. Deal with the emotional and psychological consequences of trauma to avoid long-term effects

10. Comorbidity can be used to describe a client who:

A. Is diagnosed with a terminal illness

B. Develops a medical problem that shortens the lifespan

C. Experiences suicidal ideations that result in a preoccupation with death

D. Has both mental health and Substance Use Disorders

11. A client states that she feels that she has been discriminated against at her workplace due to her sexual orientation. She is upset by this treatment and would like to find another job as she does not think that she will be successful in fighting the agency bias. The client has worked for her employer for many years without advancement and believes it is due to her marriage to another woman. In this situation it is BEST for the social worker to help the client:

A. Address the emotional consequences of discrimination

B. Find another job that will offer advancement opportunities

    C. Determine if other employees have suffered discrimination

    D. Fight the agency's discriminatory practices

12. A social worker learns that his client is a close personal friend of his supervisor. Neither the client nor the supervisor is aware of this situation. In order to address it ethically, the social worker should:

    A. Keep the circumstances confidential, not disclosing it to either the client or the supervisor

    B. Refer the client to another agency in the community

    C. Inform the client of the situation and arrange for alternate supervision within the agency

    D. Ask the client if this situation poses a problem

13. A social worker refers a client to another agency for assistance. After several months, the client returns to the social worker as she believes that the agency to which she was referred is engaging in fraudulent billing practices. The client has received notices from her insurance company that claims have been submitted and paid for services not received. In this situation, the social worker should FIRST:

    A. Ask the client for the bills and receipts to determine if the allegations are supported

    B. Provide the client with a referral to another agency

    C. Inform the client of the methods for making an official report of her stated concerns

    D. Contact the agency to determine their reasons for submitting the claims

14. A former client comes to see a social worker to get a copy of his record. As he appears to be in crisis, the social worker is concerned that he will not be able to handle the sensitive material in it, causing him harm. The social worker tells the client that it cannot be released at this time and documents her concerns in the record. This social worker's actions are:

    A. Unethical as the social worker does not know the reasons for the client's request

    B. Ethical as the client is no longer receiving services from the social worker

    C. Unethical as the client always has the right to have a copy of his record

    D. Ethical based on the competency of the client

15. A social worker has identified an ethical dilemma that exists in her agency. According to the principles of ethical problem solving, she should NEXT:

   A. Gather information on why the dilemma emerged and how long it has been present
   B. Determine whether the social work licensing board has regulations to assist with resolving it
   C. Inform her supervisor of the problem immediately to avoid negative consequences
   D. Weigh ethical issues in light of the values and principles in the professional code of ethics

16. A social worker gets a referral for a mandated client. When engaging with the client, it is MOST important for the social worker to:

   A. Ask the client what services are needed
   B. Stress that information will be kept confidential by the social worker
   C. Recognize that the client is likely ambivalent about receiving services
   D. Find out why the client has been determined to need assistance

17. When a social worker is working with a client with multiple problems, it is MOST helpful for the social worker to:

   A. Adhere closely to the steps in the problem-solving process to ensure effective treatment
   B. Remember the importance of individual dignity as a core social work value
   C. Recognize that the client must satisfy lower-level needs before moving on to meet higher-level ones
   D. Work toward establishing a therapeutic relationship built on trust and respect

18. The belief that society should be comprised of those from different social classes, religions, and races is known as:

   A. Diversity
   B. Equality
   C. Ethnocentrism
   D. Pluralism

19. When a social worker is court-mandated to disclose confidential client information without consent and such disclosure can cause harm to the client, the social worker must take all of the following actions EXCEPT:

A. Requesting that the court withdraw the court order
B. Advocating that the information released be as limited as possible
C. Asking that the records be unavailable for public inspection
D. Redacting all the harmful information prior to submitting the records to the court

20. The primary function of case management in social work is to:

A. Identify the biopsychosocial–cultural–spiritual needs of clients
B. Navigate a fragmented service delivery system
C. Make system-level changes to address societal problems
D. Cure emotional or mental dysfunction experienced by clients

21. Which of the following is TRUE about power structures in organizations?

A. Organizations have both formal and informal power structures.
B. Organizational hierarchies dictate influence in decision making.
C. Power structures in organizations are stable over time.
D. Power structures focus on making organizational changes to maximize effectiveness and efficiency.

22. A social worker notices that a client is avoiding talking about a recent visit with her family over the holiday. The social worker calls this observation to the attention of the client. The social worker is using which of the following intervention techniques?

A. Universalization
B. Clarification
C. Interpretation
D. Confrontation

23. Developing a continuum of care in social work is MOST concerned with the match between client need and service:

A. Intensity
B. Quality
C. Efficacy
D. Utilization

24. A social worker just learns that his client is the sister of his best friend. The social worker's primary concern about this situation should be focused on:

    A. Potential breaches in confidentiality
    B. The presence of a dual relationship
    C. Power differentials in the therapeutic relationship
    D. The procedures for termination

25. A client can be involuntarily committed when:

    A. The client is making poor treatment choices.
    B. The client's actions are deemed dangerous to self or others.
    C. The treatment team thinks inpatient treatment would be more effective.
    D. There are no outpatient treatment options available.

26. Separation anxiety or distress when being separated from a caregiver OFTEN begins at:

    A. 36 to 48 months
    B. 18 to 24 months
    C. 12 to 18 months
    D. 6 to 8 months

27. A client has recently had several alcohol-related arrests that a social worker believes are an indication of a substance use problem. When confronted with this possibility, the client asserts that his drinking is not an issue. This statement by the client is MOST likely caused by which of the following defense mechanisms?

    A. Rationalization
    B. Denial
    C. Projection
    D. Sublimation

28. All of the following are signs of substance abuse EXCEPT:

    A. Hiding the amount of the substance consumed
    B. Deterioration in hygiene
    C. Family history of abuse
    D. Neglecting other interests

29. Upon intake, a client reports that he has been feeling poorly and depressed about his current life situation. He has recently gained

weight and becomes easily fatigued. The client states that his feelings of hopelessness emerged about a month ago when he was diagnosed with and received a medication for a medical condition by his doctor. He has little interest in his old hobbies and feels it might be best to develop new ones. In this situation, the social worker should FIRST:

A. Conduct a suicide risk assessment
B. Gather information about his old hobbies as a way of assisting to find new ones
C. Refer him to a psychiatrist to determine if antidepressant medication is needed
D. Contact the doctor with the client's consent to discuss these emotional and physical changes

30. A client reports that her 8-year-old son can become "bossy" at times as he is constantly telling his siblings what to do around the house. He also becomes upset when consequences to discipline are not consistent. The client reports that his son likes structure in his daily routine and to have the reasons for actions explained. The client's son is MOST likely in which stage of cognitive development?

A. Formal operational
B. Concrete operational
C. Sensorimotor
D. Preoperational

31. A social worker can BEST engage in multicultural practice by:

A. Learning about the customs and traditions of the major recognized ethnic and racial groups
B. Ensuring that all service documents are translated into other languages as needed
C. Making certain that written and oral communication is bias-free
D. Acknowledging that clients are culturally diverse and define their own worldview

32. Which of the following is NOT a true statement about power in the therapeutic relationship?

A. Inherently, social workers have expert, referent, and legitimate power over clients.
B. The effectiveness of social work services is based on reducing the power differential between social workers and clients by increasing clients' resources.

C. Clients are rarely aware of the power differential that exists between themselves and social workers.

D. The power differential between social workers and clients should be openly discussed.

33. A client who was referred for psychological testing tells his social worker that the psychologist would like him to bring a copy of all pertinent information to the first appointment. In order to best address this request ethically, the social worker should:

   A. Inform the client that sharing information is prohibited by the professional code of ethics
   B. Send a copy of the entire file directly to the psychologist
   C. Provide a copy of the relevant documents to the client so that he can provide information to the psychologist as needed
   D. Wait until the psychologist contacts the social worker directly

34. Which is NOT a reason to obtain collateral information from others when working with clients?

   A. Family and friends can be helpful in providing support to resolve the problems experienced.
   B. Other informants can provide additional data on the length or severity of the issues.
   C. The credibility and validity of the information obtained from the client or other sources is questionable.
   D. Records from prior treating professionals are needed to gain insight on effective and ineffective services provided in the past.

35. A social worker is working with an adolescent girl who is very resentful toward her parents. She does not tell them when their actions upset her. Her anger has resulted in self-destructive behavior in the last month. In order to MOST effectively help this client deal with her anger, the social worker should:

   A. Determine the frequency and severity of her self-destructive actions
   B. Assess her parents' attitude about her self-destructive behavior
   C. Engage in role playing aimed at increasing her assertiveness
   D. Meet with the family to develop conflict resolution strategies

36. Which behavioral disorder is listed in the *DSM-5* under Substance-Related and Addictive Disorders?

   A. Compulsive Buying
   B. Gambling
   C. Hypersexuality
   D. Internet Gaming

37. The sandwich generation refers to those who:

   A. Rely on fast and prepared foods as their major source of nutrition
   B. Care for both children and aging parents simultaneously
   C. Experience extreme stress due to imposed work-related demands
   D. Have difficulty seeing alternative options to their problems

38. A client who is a new mother is having trouble dealing with her baby's crying. She reports becoming upset when the child cries as she "does not know what to do." The social worker can BEST assist the client by:

   A. Arranging for child care so the client has time to take care of her own needs
   B. Determining what child-care experience the client has had in the past
   C. Helping the client develop methods for soothing the child
   D. Assessing whether there are other life issues that are triggering her response

39. Which of the following is NOT true regarding spirituality and religion?

   A. Spirituality can be expressed in any religious context.
   B. Spirituality is broader than religion.
   C. Religion is encompassed within spirituality.
   D. Spirituality and religion are human experiences that provide meaning.

40. A social worker is looking at his agency's organizational chart. From this document, he is MOST likely to learn about the organization's:
   A. Mission
   B. Processes
   C. Structure
   D. History

41. Which of the statements BEST reflects the relationship between Alzheimer's disease and dementia?

    A. Alzheimer's disease can only be diagnosed if dementia is not present.
    B. Alzheimer's disease is caused by the disease of dementia.
    C. Alzheimer's disease and dementia are organic brain syndromes.
    D. Alzheimer's disease causes a set of symptoms called dementia.

42. Which of the following statements is TRUE about age of consent?

    A. Age of consent is the same in all states of the country.
    B. Age of consent is 18 years old.
    C. Most statutory rape laws historically applied only to girls.
    D. Age of consent is culturally based, with many other countries having younger ages.

43. Which of the following actions by a social worker is LEAST effective in showing empathy to a client?

    A. Using nonjudgmental verbal and nonverbal communication
    B. Listening to the client's point of view
    C. Explaining the social worker's role in the helping process
    D. Validating feelings of hopelessness in making necessary changes

44. What is the PRIMARY reason that social workers should be concerned with environmental justice?

    A. Multidisciplinary partnerships are needed to achieve environmental justice.
    B. Minority and poor communities bear the burden of environmental problems.
    C. Social workers must contribute to the available scholarly research on environmental justice.
    D. The profession must be recognized as nondiscriminatory when it comes to social justice issues.

45. In order to optimize functioning at the beginning of the group process, a social worker should:

    A. Set goals in order to guide participation throughout the process
    B. Ask group members to make decisions about their functioning as a group
    C. Select members who have homogenous cultural backgrounds
    D. Explain the purpose of the group and the rules that govern their activities

46. A social worker believes that a child is being emotionally, but not sexually or physically, abused by his mother. The social worker is probably making this assessment based on all of the following indicators EXCEPT:

    A. Interactions with others
    B. Expression of emotion
    C. Aggressive or self-harming behaviors
    D. Unexplained physical markings

47. Which of the following is NOT an essential component of a discharge plan?

    A. Presenting problem that brought client into treatment
    B. Progress made in treatment
    C. Listing of all agencies that provide ongoing treatment
    D. Services that were delivered while in treatment

48. A client has been seeing a social worker to deal with the stress of caring for her aging parents. The client is also a single mother with three small children. Since the first appointment several months ago, she has cancelled many meetings with the social worker. When next speaking with the client, the social worker should:

    A. Assess the client's level of commitment to receiving ongoing social work services
    B. Determine whether services can be delivered more conveniently
    C. Inform the client that she will be charged for missed appointments as a way of motivating her
    D. Terminate services with the understanding that she can return if needed in the future

49. When suspecting that a client is a victim of human trafficking, a social worker should FIRST focus on:

    A. Determining what circumstances led to the exploitation
    B. Helping address the emotional consequences of coercion
    C. Assessing whether the client knows of others who need assistance
    D. Finding a place where the client is safe from the perpetrator(s)

50. The MOST effective treatment for a client experiencing psychosis due to a mental illness is:

    A. Psychopharmacology
    B. Group therapy

C. Behavior management

D. Individual psychotherapy

51. A client complains to a social worker that her 12-year-old daughter recently began bedwetting after having no such issues "for years." The client states that her daughter is having no problems at home or in school and she does not know the cause of her behavior. The client is very distressed and asks the social worker for help. In order to assist, the social worker should FIRST:

A. Request a copy of the school records to determine if there are any developmental delays

B. Recommend that the client take her daughter to her physician for a medical examination

C. Meet with the daughter to see if there are problems of which the mother is not aware

D. Contact child protective services to rule out the possibility of sexual abuse

52. While doing an assessment, a social worker learns that a client's wife has recently been diagnosed with breast cancer and will begin chemotherapy immediately. Using a systems approach, the social worker can expect this diagnosis to:

A. Disrupt family homeostasis including existing role fulfillment

B. Require services to be implemented within the home

C. Necessitate long-term ongoing medical monitoring and care

D. Cause the client's wife to make adjustments to her current workload

53. Upon intake, a client appears to be sweating heavily, jittery, and shaking. The client reports that he has been a heavy drinker of alcohol for many years, but has not had a drink since yesterday. He realizes that many of his problems are caused by his alcohol use and wants help in staying sober. In order to meet his needs, the social worker should:

A. Develop a relapse prevention program aimed at avoiding his external and internal triggers

B. Refer him for a medical evaluation to address any immediate withdrawal concerns

C. Connect him with a self-help group that can provide ongoing support of his abstinence

D. Learn more about the alcohol-related problems that the client is experiencing

54. A social worker is working with a family in which both parents are chronic substance abusers. The second oldest son is always getting in trouble at school and has had several juvenile arrests. He constantly fights with his siblings. This child has MOST likely taken on the role of:

    A. Scapegoat
    B. Enabler
    C. Lost child
    D. Mascot

55. A client whose adolescent son is acting out feels that his behavior may indicate the existence of evil spirits within him. The client would like to discuss these thoughts with her spiritual leader. In order to most appropriately address the client's request, the social worker should:

    A. Advise the client that seeing her spiritual leader will not be helpful
    B. Inform the client that this behavior is typical of adolescents
    C. Work with the client to formulate her thoughts and questions for the meeting
    D. Ask the client why she thinks that evil spirits are present

56. When transference and countertransference occur in the supervisory relationship, it is known as:

    A. Universalization
    B. Differential diagnosis
    C. Parallel process
    D. Suppression

57. Delirium tremens are associated with:

    A. Parkinson's disease
    B. Alcoholism
    C. Tourette syndrome
    D. Epilepsy

58. In what area of social work practice is concurrent planning used?
    A. Mental health
    B. Substance abuse
    C. Child welfare
    D. Gerontology

59. A client has a son with a rare genetic condition that significantly limits his functional abilities. She is a single mother and feels very isolated. The client does not like to talk to her friends about her struggles and does not know anyone else in the same situation. She admits that the pressure of her caregiving responsibilities have recently caused her to engage in self-destructive behaviors such as drinking heavily, overeating, and excessive spending. In order to BEST assist the client, the social worker should recommend:

   A. Intensive individual psychotherapy to address her self-destructive behaviors
   B. A support group of others who have children with similar conditions
   C. Case management aimed at assisting her with coordinating care to reduce caregiving demands
   D. Individual and group counseling to address personal problems and provide support

60. What is the last element in case recording using a SOAP format?

   A. Process
   B. Plan
   C. Problem
   D. Prediction

61. In micro social work practice, a crisis is defined as a:

   A. Major life event that can have long-term consequences for the client's well-being
   B. Circumstance that upsets the client's steady state for which coping methods are not available or fail
   C. Physical or psychological trauma that requires long-term intervention
   D. Personal loss that can be overcome with intense and immediate services aimed at enhancing resilience

62. Which is NOT a physical sign of drug dependency?

   A. Sudden change in weight
   B. Pupil dilation or constriction
   C. Odor on breath, body, or clothing
   D. Mood swings

63. A social work administrator learns that the level of service in his organization was significantly lower this year as compared to previous years. He learns that several new agencies that serve clients with similar problems have recently opened. In this situation, the social worker should FIRST:

   A. Increase marketing efforts so that clients are aware of the services offered
   B. Evaluate the strengths, weaknesses, opportunities, and threats facing the agency
   C. Expand agency services to address other client problems
   D. Speak to the directors of the other agencies about the possibility of merging

64. Permanency planning is BEST defined as the:

   A. Process of identifying the long-term care needs of older adults in order to maximize their independence
   B. Practice philosophy that promotes a permanent living situation for those within the child welfare system
   C. Movement to build sustainable housing that is accessible to low-income individuals and families
   D. Legal procedure that appoints guardians for adults with disabilities who lack decision-making capabilities

65. Which of the following actions by a social worker is MOST effective in showing acceptance of a client who is experiencing a high degree of emotion?

   A. Asking the client about the cause of the problem
   B. Explaining to the client how the social worker can help with the situation
   C. Being silent as a way of demonstrating empathy
   D. Validating the client's feelings by stating that his or her emotions are typical

66. A client, who has recently immigrated to this country, is seeking help from a social worker due to difficulty meeting basic needs. The client appears hesitant to speak to the social worker and barely makes eye contact. The client's actions are MOST likely an indication of:

   A. Resistance to getting assistance from others
   B. Shame in asking for help

C. Anger about the current situation

D. Fear of discrimination

67. A social worker who is providing services to a married couple is asked by one member of the couple to send a copy of the record, which contains information on both parties, to a service provider to which the social worker made a referral. In order to adhere to proper confidentiality procedures, the social worker is required to get written consent from:

   A. Either member of the couple since they are legally married

   B. Neither member of the couple since it is going to another service provider

   C. Both members of the couple since the record has information on both parties

   D. Neither member of the couple since records from conjoint services cannot be released

68. When conducting a cost–benefit analysis in social work, which of the following often poses the greatest difficulty?

   A. Identifying program outcomes in fiscal terms

   B. Isolating the program costs from other agency expenses

   C. Getting client permission

   D. Determining the evaluation period

69. If a social worker is concerned about the confidentiality of information that may be ordered by the court, the social worker should request that the information be filed:

   A. Pro se

   B. Under seal

   C. Habeas corpus

   D. Using an order of protection

70. A client who gives birth after an unwanted pregnancy is an overprotective mother who talks obsessively about what she does for her child. This client's behavior is MOST likely attributable to which of the following defense mechanisms?

   A. Reaction formation

   B. Dissociation

   C. Conversion

   D. Displacement

71. When a group is so concerned with maintaining unanimity that it fails to evaluate all of its alternatives and options, it is LIKELY engaged in:

    A. Groupthink
    B. Psychodrama
    C. Interdependence
    D. Homogeneity

72. Federal antidiscrimination law prohibits discrimination based on all of the following protected classes EXCEPT:

    A. Criminal background
    B. National origin
    C. Race
    D. Disability

73. The *Tarasoff* decision mandates a social worker to report when a client:

    A. Poses a danger to an identifiable other person
    B. Abuses a child physically, emotionally, or sexually
    C. Appears at risk for hurting himself or herself
    D. Exploits or harms an elderly person

74. Which of the following statements is NOT true about the strengths perspective?

    A. Strengths-based theory is based on the assumptions that clients have the capacity to grow and adapt.
    B. Strengths can include personal attributes, family supports, community resources, and/or ethnic traditions.
    C. Confronting and addressing a stressful life situation, as well as using it as a stimulus for growth, is considered a strength.
    D. Individual strengths are consistent throughout the life course and one situation to another.

75. The goal of professional development for social workers is BEST defined as:

    A. Attaining skills and knowledge necessary for effective service delivery to clients
    B. Meeting requirements to maintain certifications and/or licenses
    C. Getting training that will assist with career advancement
    D. Achieving competency so that additional clients can be served

76. A client is very upset as her teenage son was recently arrested. The client states that she is fearful that he will "never amount to anything." The social worker had a similar experience with her child who is now grown and very successful. In order to assist the client, the social worker should:

    A. Help develop goals for the son aimed at preventing delinquency
    B. Tell the client about her own experiences as a way of instilling hope
    C. Meet with the son to find out the reasons for his troubles
    D. Ask the client about her aspirations for her son

77. Upon intake, a 23-year-old client is reluctant to reveal any information about her current living situation and provides answers that seem scripted and rehearsed. The social worker learns that she lives with many other women in very poor conditions and appears fearful when asked about how she earns money to meet her needs. The social worker feels that the woman is in danger and is a victim of human trafficking. In addition to contacting law enforcement immediately, the social worker should:

    A. Ask the client to meet with others who may be victims
    B. Contact the national human trafficking hotline
    C. Gather biopsychosocial data to assist in the investigation
    D. Offer services aimed at addressing the effects of trauma

78. A client indicates "pansexual" on an agency assessment form. Based on this information, the client is likely:

    A. To be attracted exclusively to those who are bisexual
    B. Not to be attracted to other people due to a preference to be alone
    C. To be attracted to those with varying gender and/or sexual identities
    D. Not to be attracted to those who are gender variant

79. A client reports that his young daughter just began talking. At this developmental milestone, what can the client assume to be TRUE about the relationship between her expressive and receptive language skills?
    A. The child has attained all her receptive language skills, prompting the emergence of expressive language.
    B. The child's expressive language is likely more advanced than her receptive language.

C. The child will now start to develop receptive language skills as they emerge after expressive language.
D. The child's receptive language is likely more advanced than her expressive language.

80. A social worker is meeting for the first time with a client who has recently ended a long-term relationship, is dissatisfied with her appearance, and has had trouble keeping a job. The social worker should FIRST:

A. Help the client to locate a stable job that will provide steady income
B. Ask the client why she is seeking services at this time
C. Identify the strengths that the client can use to overcome her problems
D. Complete a biopsychosocial–spiritual–cultural assessment

81. A social worker believes that a client is experiencing signs of trauma from a devastating event in his life several years ago. The most effective method for determining the existence of these symptoms is through:

A. Subjective self-reports by the client
B. Psychological testing of the client in a controlled setting
C. Objective data contained in the client's file
D. Medical evaluation of the client by a physician

82. A client has recently been prescribed lithium by his psychiatrist. The client is MOST likely to need which of the following medical tests on a routine basis?

A. Ultrasound
B. Colonoscopy
C. Blood pressure screening
D. Blood work

83. Which is NOT an activity essential to social work case management?

A. Assessing
B. Counseling
C. Linking
D. Planning

84. A client is meeting individually with a social worker to review her service plan. The client states that she is really enjoying a psychoeducation group facilitated by the social worker. However, the social worker has observed that she is frequently absent and seems disinterested when she is in attendance. The social worker should:

    A. Encourage the client to participate more in the group given her level of interest
    B. Determine what aspects of the group are most enjoyable to her
    C. Confront the client about the lack of congruence between her verbal report and her actions
    D. Assess her commitment to services as her flattering behavior may be a form of resistance

85. Somatic symptoms are defined as:

    A. Medication side effects that are not life threatening
    B. Sleep problems that are associated with mental and behavioral disorders
    C. Physical ailments that have no medical explanations
    D. Psychological stressors that cause a decrease in daily functioning

86. A client tells a social worker that she is very distressed because her 5-year-old son has an imaginary friend. She is concerned that its presence may indicate that he is lonely. In order to best assist, the social worker should:

    A. Meet with the son to determine if he is feeling isolated
    B. Ask the client if the son is experiencing any other mental health concerns
    C. Work with the client to identify ways for the son to meet other children
    D. Explain to the client about the stages of cognitive development

87. The relationship between ego strength and resiliency can BEST be defined as:

    A. Negative
    B. Positive
    C. Curvilinear
    D. Inverse

88. A client, who has made substantial progress in treatment, is in the process of termination. She starts missing appointments, which has not occurred in the past. This behavior is MOST likely an indication of:

   A. Continuation of her original problems so termination is premature
   B. Readiness to end services by placing other activities as priorities over making appointments
   C. Emergence of a new problem in the client's life that needs to be assessed
   D. Anger toward the social worker for ending the therapeutic relationship

89. The PRIMARY reason that social workers should be concerned with globalization is that it:

   A. Demands that social workers be more culturally competent
   B. Requires social workers to understand economic theories
   C. Provides opportunities for international social work practice
   D. Impacts on economic and social conditions of clients differently

90. A social worker is informed by his supervisor that services will have to be terminated to a client in a fee-for-service setting as the client has a large unpaid balance. The social worker who is upset by this decision reviews the file and sees that the client was given and signed a detailed financial contract upon intake. The social worker speaks to the client who is very upset, but not surprised, by the termination as several written warnings were received. The client is not a danger, but feels that services are beneficial to his well-being. The social worker terminates with the client, providing some alternate resources. In this situation, the social worker's actions are:

   A. Ethical as the consequences for nonpayment were made clear
   B. Unethical as the client would have continued to benefit from the services
   C. Ethical as following supervisory directives is required
   D. Unethical as the social worker did not want to terminate with the client

91. A client reports that he has recently been diagnosed with a physical disability that severely impacts his mobility. During the assessment phase, it will be MOST important for a social worker to:

   A. Understand the medical or other conditions that resulted in his limitations
   B. Establish where the client is in the human behavior and development process

C. Determine the impact of the impairment on his psychological, emotional, and social well-being

D. Identify appropriate service resources that serve those with physical disabilities

92. When assessing the impact of the cultural environment on a client, it is best for a social worker to:

A. Attend continuing education programs and seek outside resources on the subject matter

B. Consider his or her own similar personal experiences

C. Develop a culturagram when doing an assessment of the client

D. Ask others from the same ethnic background about their experiences

93. Upon intake, a social worker learns that a client is receiving medication-assisted treatment for opioid addiction. The client was MOST likely addicted to:

A. Heroin

B. Cocaine

C. Marijuana

D. Nicotine

94. A social worker finds that many of her clients are in need of behavioral services. She learns of a qualified behavioral specialist nearby to whom she agrees to refer them. The behavior specialist makes a monetary donation to the social worker's agency for additional staff training in behavior management for every referral made. This practice is:

A. Ethical as it increases the competency of staff to assist clients

B. Unethical as the behavior specialist cannot designate how the donation is used

C. Ethical as the money is not being given directly to the social worker

D. Unethical as fee splitting is prohibited

95. Which is NOT a typical stage of loss and grief?

A. Bargaining

B. Depression

C. Anger

D. Hope

96. What is the MOST essential technique used when engaged in active listening during a social work interview?

A. Mirroring
B. Questioning
C. Assessing
D. Interpreting

97. A client who was discharged about 2 months ago from the hospital after a suicide attempt has been very withdrawn and despondent while attending her partial care program. She began taking prescribed antidepressant medication when she entered the hospital and has been seeing a psychiatrist monthly. Within no more than a day, the client's spirits suddenly seem to have lifted and she appears much happier. This behavior is MOST likely resulting from:

A. Her prescribed antidepressant medications reaching therapeutic levels
B. Decreased isolation due to being around others with similar problems at her partial care program
C. The presence of suicidal risk factors that require immediate assessment
D. Feeling more comfortable with daily stressors due to the development of enhanced coping skills

98. Coping skills result from strength in which element of the personality?

A. Ego
B. Superego
C. Id
D. Preconscious

99. Resistance of clients in social work is MOST effectively regarded as:

A. Existing discretely at the onset of the problem-solving process before the therapeutic alliance develops
B. Resulting from poor performance by social workers who do not understand clients' needs
C. Providing important information that is used in accurately assessing and treating clients
D. Impeding effective service delivery so removal must occur before change can begin

100. A client reports that her son is often mistaken for a girl as he has both feminine and masculine characteristics. He has long hair and enjoys wearing makeup and jewelry. The son's appearance is described as:

    A. Transsexual
    B. Intersex
    C. Androgynous
    D. Cross dressing

101. Which of the following is NOT a potential pitfall of peer supervision?

    A. Members may not be honest about pressing service issues or learning needs.
    B. It can lack structure, without a focus on learning and evaluation.
    C. Groups may not have sufficient expertise to assist with presenting challenges.
    D. Learning is not hierarchical and relies on reciprocal sharing and self-assessment.

102. A social worker comments to his supervisor that he has a client who is a very good student. When asked about the client, the social worker states that he is smart "as expected" given that the client is Asian. The social worker's supervisor should consider this comment to be:

    A. Unacceptable as the social worker is not qualified to do intelligence testing
    B. Acceptable as cognition is a critical aspect of a thorough biopsychosocial assessment
    C. Unacceptable as it perpetuates stereotypical beliefs
    D. Acceptable as cultural considerations are being considered in making a proper assessment

103. Which of the following is true regarding life expectancy and the human lifespan?

    A. Life expectancy and the human lifespan are highly variable from one individual to another.
    B. Life expectancy of an individual is usually shorter than the human lifespan.

    C. Life expectancy of an individual and the human lifespan are always the same.

    D. Life expectancy of an individual is usually longer than the human lifespan.

104. Which of the following health conditions is NOT age related?

    A. Cerebrovascular disease

    B. Cardiovascular disease

    C. Gastroesophageal reflux disease

    D. Hypertension

105. Which theory BEST describes the interplay of biological, psychological, social, and spiritual factors to determine client well-being?

    A. Psychodynamic theory

    B. Social learning theory

    C. Systems theory

    D. Psychosocial development theory

106. A client who is diagnosed with depression is being discharged from the hospital. The client is MOST likely going to be prescribed:

    A. Haldol

    B. Lithium

    C. Prozac

    D. Clozaril

107. A social worker gets a referral from a colleague for a client who is having multiple problems. The colleague reports that the client needs to move as she is not getting along with her family and has been hospitalized for a chronic health condition. The client has a history of substance abuse and received counseling in the past. In order to best assist, it is important for the social worker to FIRST:

    A. Establish what problem(s) the client feels need immediate attention

    B. Complete a biopsychosocial–spiritual–cultural assessment

    C. Obtain records from past service providers

    D. Help the client to find alternate housing

108. A client recently revealed to a social worker that she was sexually abused by a family member as a child and that the abuse "made a real mess" of her life. In subsequent meetings, the sexual abuse was not discussed. The social worker believes that knowing more about the abuse will provide insight into her problems, but is reluctant to bring it up as the client did not appear to want to discuss it further when it was disclosed. In this situation, the social worker should:

- **A.** Wait until the client mentions the sexual abuse again and use it as an opening to inquire about it further
- **B.** Ask the client open-ended nonthreatening questions about the sexual abuse
- **C.** Complete a sexual history to find out how the sexual abuse may have impacted development
- **D.** Tell the client that the sexual abuse and its effects are not her fault

109. Which of the following is NOT a maturational crisis?

- **A.** Puberty
- **B.** Marriage
- **C.** Child death
- **D.** Retirement

110. Upon intake, a social worker learns that a client has a significant hearing impairment. She typically uses American Sign Language (ASL) to communicate, but has the ability to hear amplified speech. The client is seeking assistance as she recently experienced reductions in her benefits. She believes these changes resulted from her inability to communicate her circumstances to others. As there are no certified ASL interpreters on staff at the agency, the client states that she can find a family member or friend to assist in translating. The social worker should:

- **A.** Help the client make contact with the person who can assist immediately
- **B.** Conduct the interview speaking loudly since the client is able to hear amplified speech
- **C.** Inform the client that her needs cannot be met at the agency and refer her elsewhere
- **D.** Arrange for a qualified interpreter to be present at the next meeting

111. A social worker is starting a new program in his agency and would like to do ongoing evaluation during implementation in order to make modifications aimed at increasing its efficiency and effectiveness. Which of the following evaluations is BEST suited for this purpose?

    A. Formative
    B. Quasi-experimental
    C. Summative
    D. Experimental

112. In social work, best practice standards, including those related to confidentiality, dictate that the contents of client records should:

    A. Reflect summaries which do not contain information that can be harmful if released
    B. Contain only relevant detailed information for service continuity and evaluation
    C. Omit opinions about current functioning and prognosis for change
    D. Include disclosures about the safeguards in place to protect electronic health records

113. When program eligibility is determined by means testing, continued service relies on:

    A. Making progress toward goals
    B. Complying with program rules
    C. Remaining financially qualified
    D. Attending services regularly

114. Termination in the problem-solving process should include all of the following tasks EXCEPT:

    A. Anticipating future
    B. Acknowledging loss
    C. Reviewing accomplishments
    D. Reiterating confidentiality standards

115. Which statement supports the use of cognitive restructuring with clients?

    A. Thoughts are often not supported by empirical evidence.
    B. Trauma can cause lasting physical and emotional effects.

    C. Mental disorders need to be diagnosed and treated to promote well-being.

    D. Change can only occur if there is a readiness to approach problems differently.

116. During assessment, a social worker learns that a client feels isolated as she is recently retired and is struggling to meet others. Her workplace had provided a venue for socialization and support. She feels that these elements in her life are missing since she is no longer employed. In formulating a service plan, the client's needs are BEST met through the provision of:

    A. Vocational services

    B. Case management

    C. Individual counseling

    D. Group participation

117. When developing a document ordered by the court, the primary concern of a social worker should be ensuring that the report:

    A. Contains as little information as possible to protect client confidentiality

    B. Is submitted in a timely manner to avoid penalties to both the social worker and client

    C. Includes relevant concise information that is based on objective client assessment

    D. Does not result in negative consequences that will adversely affect client well-being

118. Under federal law, which of the following is NOT a criterion for the definition of a developmental disability?

    A. Manifesting before age 18

    B. Likely to continue indefinitely

    C. Resulting in substantial limitations in three or more major life areas

    D. Reflecting the need for special, interdisciplinary, individualized, or other services

119. The PRIMARY reason that there are three distinct branches of government is to:

    A. Separate powers so that there are checks and balances

    B. Get more citizens involved in the policy-making process

    C. Ensure that there are adequate financial resources to operate effectively

    D. Make operations more transparent to the public

120. A social worker finds that she has a lot in common with a client. The client reports that she is often lonely as she has few friends with which to socialize. The client asks the social worker if they could do things together if services ended. The social worker and client agree to work together to find another appropriate service provider. After ensuring that the client is satisfied with the new arrangement, the social worker terminates services. Several weeks later, the social worker invites the client to go shopping with her. In this situation, the social worker's actions are:

    A. Ethical as it was the client's desire to end the services

    B. Unethical as termination was inappropriate in this situation

    C. Ethical as the socialization did not start occurring until the therapeutic relationship ended

    D. Unethical as more time should have passed after termination before socializing with the client

121. A client reports that he grew up in a culture in which men were viewed as authority figures and made all decisions within families. Such a social system is defined as:

    A. Democratic

    B. Pluralistic

    C. Egalitarian

    D. Patriarchal

122. During the assessment phase, a client reports growing up in a large immediate and extended family that influenced his current life situation. In order to understand the family structure and relationships, the social worker can best be assisted by the use of a:

    A. Biopsychosocial–spiritual–cultural assessment

    B. Personality test

    C. Genogram

    D. Psychiatric evaluation

123. A client tells a social worker that he has designated a power of attorney. Which of the following does the social worker know to be true about the client based on this information?

    A. The client is incompetent to make legal and medical choices for himself.
    B. The client has made decisions about to whom he will be leaving his assets after his death.
    C. The client has designated someone else to make decisions for him if needed.
    D. The client is involved in a legal matter and has retained a lawyer to represent him.

124. A social worker, having problems settling his father's estate, discloses this information to his client, who is a lawyer. The client suggests some legal forms that will resolve the matter. The social worker's actions PRIMARILY raise concerns about:

    A. Boundaries
    B. Confidentiality
    C. Informed consent
    D. Payment

125. Understanding human development is MOST important for social workers because it:

    A. Determines whether clients should be diagnosed with developmental delays
    B. Illustrates the effects of the environment on client system behavior
    C. Demonstrates the cultural differences that exist between different client groups
    D. Helps explain the predictable growth progression that most clients will experience

126. Definitive diagnoses of Alzheimer's disease are BEST made by:

    A. Blood work upon onset of symptoms
    B. Brain biopsies after death
    C. Medical examinations on adults over age 65
    D. Genetic testing on those with hereditary predispositions

127. A social worker is working with an adolescent client who is having trouble talking to his parents about problems at home. He tells the social worker that he does not know what to say to them about his frustrations. In order to enhance the client's communication skills, the social worker should:

   A. Use role playing to assist the client with effectively expressing his emotions
   B. Ask the client about past interactions with his parents that may have inhibited communication
   C. Determine the nature of the problems to assess whether a family meeting is warranted
   D. Arrange for a family session so that the client can bring up his concerns

128. A social work administrator interested in assessing the job satisfaction of agency employees asks them on a survey, "How satisfied are you with your pay and job conditions?" The social worker allows employees to answer using a Likert scale of very satisfied, satisfied, neutral, unsatisfied, or very unsatisfied. Which BEST defines the concern with use of this question?

   A. Results may not provide accurate information about employee satisfaction and concerns.
   B. It is inappropriate to ask about compensation as the social work administrator has no control over wages offered.
   C. There should be more response choices available to employees in order to assess their satisfaction more precisely.
   D. The employees should decide whether the question is included on the survey.

129. A social worker is worried about the growing tension between an adolescent client and his parents. The social worker looks through case notes written over the past 6 months to determine whether client concerns have resulted from increasing conflict. The social worker's assessment is based on the underlying themes of client communication rather than specific words used. This review focuses on:

   A. Reflective interviewing
   B. Manifest content
   C. Nonverbal cues
   D. Latent communication

130. According to the professional code of ethics, a social worker who reports a client as an alleged perpetrator of child abuse should:

  A. Inform the client about the mandatory need to inform the child protection agency
  B. Never tell the client about the report being made in order to protect the safety of the child
  C. Follow agency policy when making decisions about disclosing the report to the client
  D. Disclose that the report was made only after the investigation is completed

131. Tertiary prevention for children who have been abused is important in the reduction of child abuse as:

  A. Victims deserve to have offenders punished for their crimes.
  B. Offenders are much more likely to be victims of child maltreatment.
  C. Many incidences of child abuse are not reported to authorities.
  D. Society should be knowledgeable about the effects of all forms of abuse.

132. Compassion fatigue is BEST defined as:

  A. Physical exhaustion associated with working long hours in dangerous situations
  B. A syndrome that results from the chronic use of empathy with those in need
  C. Psychological problems that result from prioritizing the needs of others over self-care
  D. Psychosomatic exhaustion aimed at eliciting compassion from others

133. The debate about the degree to which biological versus environmental variables impact on development is known as:

  A. Medical versus sociological
  B. Nature versus nurture
  C. Determinism versus free will
  D. Rationalism versus empiricism

134. What is the PRIMARY reason that using recurrent substance-related legal problems is not a good criterion for diagnosing substance use issues?

   A. Clients rarely are honest about their legal troubles.
   B. Substance-related arrests do not always result in convictions.
   C. Legal involvement is impacted by race and economic factors.
   D. Legal problems include a diverse set of criminal behaviors.

135. A client who was previously diagnosed as having Mental Retardation would likely be identified as having:

   A. Autism Spectrum Disorder
   B. Intellectual Developmental Disorder
   C. Attention-Deficit/Hyperactivity Disorder
   D. Specific Learning Disorder

136. A school social worker who regularly meets with an adolescent client learns that she is experiencing many problems. She is doing poorly academically and is at risk for not moving on to the next grade. The client states that it is difficult to do her homework as she has to take care of her siblings. Her mother recently went back to work as the family risks homelessness. The social worker can most effectively understand the current situation by:

   A. Speaking with the teachers to see if time can be made for her to do her homework while at school
   B. Conducting a biopsychosocial assessment using school records as collateral data sources
   C. Meeting with the client and her family, as well as the teachers, to discuss the presenting problems
   D. Examining her academic history to determine whether her performance declined as her domestic responsibilities increased

137. When mandated to release confidential information in order to comply with a court order, a social worker should:

   A. Inform the client of the disclosure and its consequences before submitting the information
   B. Keep the court order confidential from the client as required by law
   C. Send a copy of the court order to the client immediately so the request is known
   D. Obtain a lawyer for representation during future legal proceedings

138. Which of the following characteristics is NOT valued in collectivistic cultures?

    A. Generosity
    B. Helpfulness
    C. Dependability
    D. Independence

139. Which of the following is the best method for assessing a client's gender identity?

    A. Examining the client's medical records
    B. Interviewing the client directly
    C. Observing the client in interactions with others
    D. Reviewing psychological testing done on the client

140. A social worker believes that an 8-year-old client is being physically abused at home. The client tells the social worker that he was "beat up" by a cousin who has since moved out of the home. In this situation, the social worker should:

    A. Speak to a supervisor about the suspected abuse
    B. Monitor the situation closely for any further signs of abuse
    C. Make a report to the child protection agency
    D. Tell the client that he should always be truthful with the social worker

141. Which of the following is NOT likely to increase cohesion within groups?

    A. Heterogeneity among members
    B. Smaller size
    C. A closed structure
    D. Member involvement in goal setting

142. A client reports that her son's school is concerned about his developmental delays. At a recent evaluation, the child was asked to pick up buttons from a table and put them into a cup. This task is MOST likely used to assess:

    A. Expressive communication skills
    B. Fine motor skills
    C. Social skills
    D. Gross motor skills

143. A social worker is hired to work in a school for youth with developmental disabilities. When reviewing the record of a student with Down syndrome, the social worker is MOST likely going to see the results of which of the following tests?

    A. Wechsler Intelligence Scale
    B. Minnesota Multiphasic Personality Inventory
    C. Beck Depression Inventory
    D. Thematic Apperception Test

144. A social worker believes that a client is falsifying and exaggerating physical symptoms. In order for this behavior to be considered malingering, the behavior must result in:

    A. Impaired long-term functioning of the client
    B. Reward or benefit for the client
    C. Problems in the client's interpersonal relationships
    D. Enhanced self-image through client assuming a sick role

145. When addressing conflict within interdisciplinary teams, it is MOST important for social workers to remember that team members:

    A. Come from different personal and professional cultural backgrounds
    B. Must be able to effectively work together in order to achieve desired outcomes
    C. Should have clients' best interests guiding their decisions
    D. Need to put their personal differences aside when doing their work

146. Which of the following is NOT a justification for the provision of respite for parents of children with developmental disabilities?

    A. The positive well-being of parents is essential to the provision of quality care to their children.
    B. Children with developmental disabilities should receive early intervention services.
    C. It is best for children to grow up in homes with parents who are the primary caregivers.
    D. Caring for children with developmental disabilities can be more difficult and stressful.

147. Using the problem-solving approach, when does assessment of a client occur?

    A. Immediately after engagement has occurred
    B. Throughout the entire helping process
    C. When an intervention plan is being developed
    D. Following the collection of biopsychosocial information

148. When a social worker is assisting a client who is upset when trying to stay sober after a recent relapse, the immediate goal should be to:

    A. Identify the external and internal triggers that caused the client to relapse
    B. Access supports aimed at promoting continued abstinence
    C. Get a long-term commitment from the client for continued sobriety
    D. Help the client deal with the emotional shame that can accompany relapse

149. A social worker receives a subpoena from the court for records of a former client. Wanting to protect the client's confidentiality to the extent legally possible, the social worker prepares a written summary of the presenting problems, services delivered, and discharge plan. This summary, instead of the records, is then sent to the court by the social worker. This social worker's actions are:

    A. Unethical as the social worker had an ethical and legal duty to submit the entire record to the court
    B. Ethical as the client minimized the amount of information disclosed while still complying with the law
    C. Unethical as the social worker should have claimed privilege and not submitted any client information
    D. Ethical as the client is no longer receiving services and does not have the same rights to confidentiality

150. When social workers are working with clients who lack capacity to provide informed consent, which of the following is NOT mandated by the professional code of ethics?

    A. Consent for services should be obtained by appropriate third parties.
    B. Clients should be informed consistent with their level of understanding.

C. Reasonable steps should be made to safeguard clients' interests and rights.

D. Competency must be reevaluated to ensure that clients are not able to legally make decisions.

151. A client who has Schizophrenia is MOST likely to have which type of hallucinations?

   A. Auditory
   B. Visual
   C. Tactile
   D. Olfactory

152. A client who was recently beaten by her husband reports that he is very remorseful and has been attentive to her needs. Based on the cycle of abuse, there will be:

   A. A phase of tension building followed by further battering
   B. No further incidents of violence in their relationship
   C. Continued contrition that dictates whether physical abuse will occur in the future
   D. Greater danger if the relationship is ended at this time

153. What is the PRIMARY client benefit of receiving group as opposed to individual services?

   A. Group services require less staff time so they can be implemented more easily.
   B. Group services are usually less expensive and, therefore, more accessible to clients.
   C. Group services provide natural peer support to clients, reducing isolation.
   D. Group services allow members to make decisions with regard to their care.

154. Cisgender is used to describe those whose gender identities:

   A. Conform with the gender they were assigned at birth
   B. Diverge from traditional binary gender classifications
   C. Change from male to female over their life course
   D. Do not match the gender they were assigned at birth

155. A client is discussing her concerns about an upcoming medical procedure with a social worker. The client has been ordered to have an electroencephalography (EEG) by her doctor to assist in diagnosing some recent health problems. She is fearful of needles and has a low tolerance for pain. The BEST way that a social worker can assist is to:

  A. Contact her doctor to see if a sedative can be prescribed to reduce her anxiety
  B. Provide some biofeedback techniques for her to use when having the procedure
  C. Complete a biopsychosocial assessment to determine the impact of her medical problems on her mental health
  D. Explain in detail what she can expect when having this procedure in an attempt to allay her fears

156. A client states that she is having frequent episodes of anxiety and does not know what is causing them. In order to properly identify the client's need, the social worker should:

  A. Understand the client's family relationships and history
  B. Gather collateral information from others who may be knowledgeable
  C. Assess the client's existing coping skills to deal with stress
  D. Determine the antecedents and frequency of the episodes

157. Which of the following needs is NOT considered a deficiency need?

  A. Physiological
  B. Self-actualization
  C. Safety
  D. Esteem

158. A social worker learns from a client that she will have to leave her house due to foreclosure in the next few days. She is having financial troubles but would like to be able to remain in her house by renting it from the new owner. The bank has told her that it will be sold for far less than its assessed value, but they have no control over whether the new owner would rent to her. The client is deeply troubled by having to move. The social worker agrees to contact the bank with the intent of purchasing the home as an investment property and renting it back to the client. The social worker's actions are:

  A. Unethical unless the arrangement is done with the informed consent of the client
  B. Ethical as the actions prevent the client from becoming homeless

    C. Unethical due to a conflict of interest

    D. Ethical as long as the client is charged only fair market rent

159. The concept that the same end can result from many potential means is known as:

    A. Equifinality

    B. Throughput

    C. Entropy

    D. Homeostasis

160. A social worker finds that she is experiencing distress associated with burnout. In order to appropriately deal with this situation, the social worker should:

    A. Seek professional help and adjust workloads to protect clients and others

    B. Identify the main causes of the burnout so that they can be addressed by the agency

    C. Consult with her supervisor to determine whether remedial action is needed

    D. Continue to monitor the situation to ensure that it does not interfere with her practice

161. Which of the following statements is TRUE about childhood sexual abuse?

    A. Children who are abused immediately report the abuse to their parents or others.

    B. Well-educated, middle class adults are rarely perpetrators of abuse.

    C. Child molesters do not abuse all children with whom they come in contact.

    D. Children who are abused will show physical evidence of their molestation.

162. A social worker has a client who runs away repeatedly from her mother's home. Based on this behavior, the social worker writes that the client is "self-reliant and independent" in an evaluation. The social worker is using which of the following perspectives in making the assessment?

    A. Strengths

    B. Feminist

    C. Conflict
    D. Rational choice

163. What is a significant concern when a social worker repeatedly treats the same client system need in the same setting?

    A. The social worker is more likely to burnout due to inadequate supports.
    B. The social worker cannot learn new skills and knowledge to assist in career progression.
    C. The social worker will not consider the differences in clients that may impact service delivery.
    D. The social worker has a limited peer group of professionals to provide consultation.

164. The self-medication hypothesis to explain the high comorbidity between Substance Use Disorders and mental illness is BEST supported by which statement?

    A. Substance abuse and mental illness both result from hereditary predispositions.
    B. The use of drugs can have long-term physical and emotional effects.
    C. Substance abuse and mental illness are more prevalent in those who have experienced trauma.
    D. Symptoms of mental disorders may be lessened by the use of drugs.

165. When obtaining collateral information in order to complete assessments, which of the following is TRUE about social workers' need for informed consent from clients?

    A. Informed consent is needed prior to contacting collateral sources.
    B. Informed consent is needed when other professionals are contacted, but not when family and friends are used as collateral contacts.
    C. Informed consent is not needed to gather collateral information from other sources.
    D. Informed consent is only needed if written documents are obtained, but not when verbal information is gathered as part of the problem-solving process.

166. Insurance companies control costs and monitor quality of care through:

   A. Capitated billing
   B. Utilization review
   C. Level of care determinations
   D. Peer grouping

167. Which of the following statements is TRUE about sexuality in older adulthood?

   A. Older adults do not have to worry about contracting sexually transmitted diseases.
   B. Older adults experience physical changes that can lead to sexual problems.
   C. Older adults experience sexual dissatisfaction as a result of the aging process.
   D. Older adults, especially women, are not interested in sexual activity.

168. A client has decided to drop out of college to take care of her boyfriend's mother. The social worker feels that the client is making a poor choice as there are other available supports for the mother's care. When speaking with the client about her decision, the social worker must:

   A. Acknowledge that she has the right to make her own choices
   B. Explain the other options that are available to meet the mother's needs
   C. Inform her that there is a risk that she will not return to college if she drops out now
   D. Determine whether the boyfriend is pressuring her to make this decision

169. Which of the following is NOT one of the primary functions of supervision?

   A. Administrative
   B. Evaluative
   C. Educational
   D. Supportive

170. Which of the following BEST describes the ethical mandates of social workers with regard to political action?

   A. Social workers should not engage in political action in order to ensure bipartisan support for human service programs.

   B. Social workers should be informed of political action strategies that promote the visibility of the profession and its mission.

   C. Social workers have no professional ethical mandates to engage in political action, making it an individual choice.

   D. Social workers should engage in political action and the political arena in order to promote social justice.

Answer Key

1. A	18. D	35. C	52. A
2. C	19. D	36. B	53. B
3. D	20. B	37. B	54. A
4. C	21. A	38. C	55. C
5. B	22. D	39. D	56. C
6. A	23. A	40. C	57. B
7. D	24. B	41. D	58. C
8. C	25. B	42. D	59. D
9. B	26. D	43. C	60. B
10. D	27. B	44. B	61. B
11. D	28. C	45. B	62. D
12. C	29. D	46. D	63. B
13. C	30. B	47. C	64. B
14. D	31. D	48. B	65. C
15. D	32. C	49. D	66. B
16. C	33. C	50. A	67. C
17. C	34. A	51. B	68. A

69. B	95. D	121. D	147. B
70. A	96. A	122. C	148. B
71. A	97. C	123. C	149. C
72. A	98. A	124. A	150. D
73. A	99. C	125. D	151. A
74. D	100. C	126. B	152. A
75. A	101. D	127. A	153. C
76. D	102. C	128. A	154. A
77. B	103. B	129. D	155. D
78. C	104. C	130. A	156. D
79. D	105. C	131. B	157. B
80. B	106. C	132. B	158. C
81. A	107. A	133. B	159. A
82. D	108. B	134. C	160. A
83. B	109. C	135. B	161. C
84. C	110. D	136. C	162. A
85. C	111. A	137. A	163. C
86. D	112. B	138. D	164. D
87. B	113. C	139. B	165. A
88. B	114. D	140. C	166. B
89. D	115. A	141. A	167. B
90. A	116. D	142. B	168. A
91. C	117. C	143. A	169. B
92. C	118. A	144. B	170. D
93. A	119. A	145. A	
94. D	120. B	146. B	

Answers With Analytic Rationales

1. A

Rationale

This client is likely in middle adulthood and is faced with the challenge of understanding himself as part of the larger society. During this time, adults strive to create or nurture things that will outlast them—often by having children or contributing to positive changes that benefit other people. According to Erik Erikson, contributing to society and doing things to benefit future generations are important needs at the **generativity versus stagnation stage** of development. Generativity refers to "making your mark" on the world through caring for others, creating things, and accomplishing things that make the world a better place. Stagnation refers to the failure to find a way to contribute, leaving individuals feeling disconnected or uninvolved with their community and with society as a whole.

Test-Taking Strategies Applied

The question begins with several sentences about the client's past and current life experiences, including his current desire to "make a difference by giving back." Material in quotation marks deserves particular attention and usually relates to the answer. One other answer relates to helping others by teaching, but it does not account for the qualifying word—MOST. Erikson described generativity versus stagnation as part of psychosocial development for all in middle adulthood.

Knowledge Area

Unit I—Human Development, Diversity, and Behavior in the Environment (Content Area); Human Growth and Development

(Competency); Theories of Human Development Throughout the Lifespan (e.g., Physical, Social, Emotional, Cognitive, Behavioral) (KSA)

2. C

Rationale

Reliability is related to the consistency of data collected. When using observers to collect information, there is always a concern about whether results are reliable or consistent. Observers can be distracted or simply miss critical interactions. In order to determine whether all data were gathered consistently, **interobserver reliability** (the use of independent observers to see whether they record the same events) is needed. The social worker in this case scenario is using this approach by having a colleague independently observe interactions so that she can compare results.

There are other types of reliability testing—such as test–retest reliability (assessing the consistency of a measure from one time to another), parallel-forms reliability (comparing results of two tests assessing the same domain), and internal consistency reliability (examining the consistency of results across items within a test).

Test-Taking Strategies Applied

The question contains a qualifying word—MOST. While all of the response choices contain research terms, the use of independent observers relates to concerns with consistency or reliability of the data being gathered.

Knowledge Area

Unit III—Interventions With Clients/Client Systems (Content Area); Intervention Processes and Techniques (Competency); Methods, Techniques, and Instruments Used to Evaluate Social Work Practice (KSA)

3. D

Rationale

Development is the series of **age-related changes** that happen over the course of a lifespan. Several famous psychologists, including Sigmund Freud, Erik Erikson, Jean Piaget, and Lawrence Kohlberg, describe development as a series of stages. A stage is a period in development in which people exhibit typical behavior patterns and establish particular capacities. Age-stage developmental theorists view these age-related stages as discrete and occurring in sequential order.

While the last response choice may be true, it is NOT a hallmark of age-stage development theories.

Test-Taking Strategies Applied

The question contains a qualifying word—NOT—that requires social workers to select the response choice which is not a tenet of age-stage developmental theories. When NOT is used as a qualifying word, it is often helpful to remove it from the question and eliminate the three response choices that *are* essential components of age-stage development. This approach will leave the one response choice which is NOT an assumption.

Knowledge Area

Unit I—Human Development, Diversity, and Behavior in the Environment (Content Area); Human Growth and Development (Competency); Theories of Human Development Throughout the Lifespan (e.g., Physical, Social, Emotional, Cognitive, Behavioral) (KSA)

4. C

Rationale

In operant conditioning, behavior is reinforced by either gaining something positive or having something negative taken away when the behavior occurs. **Extinction** is the disappearance of a previously learned behavior when the behavior is not reinforced. For example, if a child always gets what he or she wants from a parent after having a tantrum, it is likely that these tantrums will persist because they are being reinforced. However, if the parent does not provide the desired response after a tantrum, the tantrums will likely subsist over time. This process is known as extinction.

Test-Taking Strategies Applied

This is a recall question that relies on social workers understanding behavioral interventions and key terms associated with these interventions. The question is seeking the name of a behavioral technique used to stop an action. However, even without in-depth knowledge of behavioral management principles, it is possible to identify extinction as a disappearance. For example, species that are extinct no longer exist. Thus, critically thinking about the meaning of the words provided as answers could assist in picking out the correct response.

Knowledge Area

Unit I—Human Development, Diversity, and Behavior in the Environment (Content Area); Human Growth and Development (Competency); Theories of Human Development Throughout the Lifespan (e.g., Physical, Social, Emotional, Cognitive, Behavioral) (KSA)

5. B

Rationale

Residual welfare is essentially seen as being in place purely for those who are poorer in society, providing a safety net for them. Social work becomes "residual" when it is reactive or gap-filling. It only provides assistance when all other efforts and measures concerning natural resources have been depleted—support from family, religious institutions, and so on.

   Institutional welfare practice takes the approach that needs are a part of everyday life and that welfare should be provided as a public service. Institutional social work focuses on giving each person equal opportunity to be supported, whatever his or her circumstances.

   Supplemental nutrition assistance is based on a residual approach as it is only available to those who are low income. The Supplemental Nutrition Assistance Program (SNAP) is the largest program in the domestic hunger safety net and was formerly known as Food Stamps. Public education, law enforcement, and Social Security are available to all citizens, regardless of income or condition.

Test-Taking Strategies Applied

This is a recall question that relies on social workers understanding the differences between social welfare approaches. An important word is "residual," meaning that which remains or is left behind.

   The safety net, which includes supplemental nutrition assistance, is for those who are not able to meet their basic needs or are disenfranchised (i.e., left behind). Thus, critically thinking about the meaning of "residual" could assist in picking out the correct response.

Knowledge Area

Unit III—Interventions With Clients/Client Systems (Content Area); Intervention Processes and Techniques (Competency); The Effects of Policies, Procedures, Regulations, and Legislation on Social Work Practice and Service Delivery (KSA)

6. A

Rationale

Rationalization is a cognitive distortion to make an event or an impulse less threatening. It makes this event or impulse more acceptable. The client is providing a more comfortable explanation to explain her termination, though it is not the reason for her firing.

Displacement is the redirection of an impulse to a less threatening target. The target can be a person or an object that can serve as a symbolic substitute. **Projection** involves individuals attributing their own thoughts, feelings, and motives to another person. Thoughts most commonly projected onto another are the ones that would cause guilt. **Conversion** is when a repressed urge is manifested in disturbance of a body function, such as deafness, blindness, paralysis, and so on.

Test-Taking Strategies Applied

The question contains a qualifying word—MOST. It is possible that the client could be using projection by attributing her own jealousy of her boss to her supervisor.

However, the third sentence in the case scenario must be considered. It describes poor performance, which is not acknowledged by the client. The inability to consider her tardiness and poor performance as the basis for her firing is an indication that the client is MOST likely rationalizing these actions.

Knowledge Area

Unit I—Human Development, Diversity, and Behavior in the Environment (Content Area); Human Behavior in the Social Environment (Competency); Psychological Defense Mechanisms and Their Effects on Behavior and Relationships (KSA)

7. D

Rationale

Consultation is done by those who have specialized knowledge or expertise, often in areas in which organizational workers have knowledge gaps. Consultation is usually time limited, aiming at solving specific problems identified by organizations and their employees. It can be done for free, but is usually associated with a fee related to the education and skill levels of those serving as consultants. However, these fees are not always high.

Consultants have no formal authority within organizations, but they usually have informal power based upon the high regard given to their advice. Organizations do not need to follow the recommendations of consultants, which are considered advisory. The ultimate decision of whether to implement a consultant's advice rests with organizational decision makers.

Supervision is not done solely by generalists or those with broad areas of knowledge. In addition, supervision is usually ongoing, whereas consultation is not. Supervisors within organizations have formal authority over employees—meaning they have the ability to hire, fire, and make other sanctioned decisions.

Based on this information, only the last response choice is true of both consultants and supervisors.

Test-Taking Strategies Applied

The question contains a qualifying word—BOTH. Its use indicates that some of the response choices may contain accurate information about either one of the two roles, but only one is true about both. It is critical to be able to tease out what is being stated about consultants and supervisors separately in each of the response choices and weigh its accuracy. Only the response choice with factual assertions related to both is correct.

Knowledge Area

Unit IV—Professional Relationships, Values, and Ethics (Content Area); Professional Development and Use of Self (Competency); Models of Supervision and Consultation (e.g., Individual, Peer, Group) (KSA)

8. C

Rationale

The purpose of **licensing and certification in social work** is to protect the public through identification of standards for the safe professional practice of social work. Each jurisdiction defines by law what requisite knowledge and education are required for social work licensure. Regulatory bodies overseeing social work licensure:

- Establish the rules and regulations of the profession and the standards for licensure
- Issue licenses to those who have met these professional standards
- Investigate complaints and, when necessary, decide what actions are needed or whether social workers should continue to practice

Impacts on or raising of the salaries of social workers is not a stated purpose of licensure.

Test-Taking Strategies Applied

The question contains a qualifying word—NOT—that requires social workers to select the response choice that is not an intended purpose of social work licensure. When NOT is used as a qualifying word, it is often helpful to remove it from the question and eliminate the three response choices that *are* functions of licensure. This approach will leave the one response choice that is NOT a reason.

Knowledge Area

Unit IV—Professional Relationships, Values, and Ethics (Content Area); Professional Development and Use of Self (Competency); Professional Development Activities to Improve Practice and Maintain Current Professional Knowledge (e.g., In-Service Training, Licensing Requirements, Reviews of Literature, Workshops) (KSA)

9. B

Rationale

Crisis intervention is a process of actively influencing the psychosocial functioning of clients during a period of disequilibrium or crisis. It focuses on the here-and-now and requires a high level of involvement. The focus of crisis intervention must be immediate assistance to alleviate stress caused by presenting problems. Other foci will be viewed as nonresponsive by the client. In addition, implementing preventive measures and strategies for handling future strategies can be done after the client has returned to his or her previous level of functioning or regained equilibrium. Addressing the long-term effects are important, but not the main focus of crisis intervention.

Test-Taking Strategies Applied

The question contains a qualifying word—primary—though it is not capitalized. Its inclusion indicates that crisis intervention may address more than one of the aims stated, but the main purpose must be selected from the rest. A key word in the correct response choice is "immediate." Crisis intervention must address immediate needs or presenting problems.

Knowledge Area

Unit III—Interventions With Clients/Client Systems (Content Area); Intervention Processes and Techniques (Competency); Crisis Intervention and Treatment Approaches (KSA)

10. D

Rationale

Comorbidity occurs when a client has conditions or diagnoses which occur simultaneously. For example, a client may possess a physical illness and mental health problem. In addition, a client would be considered to have comorbid conditions if he or she had two or more distinct mental health diagnoses.

In the last response choice, a client has two simultaneous issues— mental health and Substance Use Disorders—making them comorbid.

Test-Taking Strategies Applied

"Morbid" indicates an unhealthy state or the indication of disease. Many of the response choices address the presence of illness or thoughts of death. However, only the correct answer considers the use of "co-," which means *joint* or *together*. Thus, the correct response choice has to contain more than one disabling condition or attitude.

Knowledge Area

Unit II—Assessment (Content Area); Biopsychosocial History and Collateral Data (Competency); The Indicators of Mental and Emotional Illness Throughout the Lifespan (KSA)

11. D

Rationale

Social workers are charged with not only dealing with the effects of discrimination, but also making macro-level changes that correct the injustice. While the client's emotional well-being is important, it will not result in changes that will prevent such discrimination from occurring again. Utilizing an empowerment approach will be most helpful. **Advocacy to end discriminatory practices** can take many forms, including directly fighting the biases or eliciting the assistance of a rights organization to assist or take the lead. The social worker can take the actions listed in the incorrect response choices, but only fighting the discrimination addresses the root cause of the problem.

Test-Taking Strategies Applied

The question contains a qualifying word—BEST. While some of the response choices may be useful to the client, they do not address the root cause of the problem. Remembering the ethical mandate to end discriminatory practices or policies is useful when answering this question. Social workers should not only address the effects of problems, but help clients make personal and systemic changes that will prevent them from occurring in the future.

Knowledge Area

Unit I—Human Development, Diversity, and Behavior in the Environment (Content Area); Diversity, Social/Economic Justice, and Oppression (Competency); Systemic (Institutionalized) Discrimination (e.g., Racism, Sexism, Ageism) (KSA)

12. C

Rationale

A social worker should be alert to and avoid **conflicts of interest** that interfere with the exercise of professional discretion and impartial judgment. A social worker must inform the client when any real or potential conflict arises and take reasonable steps to resolve the issue in a manner that makes a client's interest primary and protects a client's interest to the greatest extent possible. Thus, not disclosing the situation to the client is inappropriate.

In some cases, protecting a client's interest may require termination of a professional relationship with proper referral of the client to another agency. However, this decision should not be unilaterally made by the social worker without discussion with the client. If alternate supervision is available, it may be possible for the client not to have to start over with a social worker at another agency. The social worker should not have begun providing services to this client if this conflict of interest was known. Once such a conflict is evident, action must be taken by the social worker.

Test-Taking Strategies Applied

The question requires that the situation be addressed *ethically*. Two of the response choices do not include any definitive action by the social worker. Referral to another agency may not need to occur unless the client feels it is necessary. The social worker can keep the identity of the client confidential from the supervisor and still get needed supervision by speaking directly to the agency director. It is essential that the client understands the situation and feels comfortable with the remedy because the client may feel betrayed by the social worker—even if alternate supervision was provided—when learning that the friend has a supervisory relationship with the social worker. The client may worry that confidential information was discussed.

Knowledge Area

Unit IV—Professional Relationships, Values, and Ethics (Content Area); Professional Values and Ethical Issues (Competency); Ethical Issues Related to Dual Relationships (KSA)

13. C

Rationale

Social workers often need to make referrals to other service providers. They have a responsibility with regard to **provider competency**. In addition, social workers must follow up to make sure providers are meeting clients' needs.

In this case scenario, it is not the social worker's responsibility to investigate the allegations and make a determination of their validity. Although a referral to another agency may be warranted, the client is coming back to the social worker because of concerns about billing, which must be addressed in the correct response choice. The social worker should not be contacting the agency to determine their justification for submitting the claims.

Supporting the client by providing education about the available alternatives for reporting is the most appropriate answer. Once the suspicion is reported, the client may learn information from the insurance company that provides legitimate reasoning for such claims, causing the client to want to remain with the agency. Conversely, the client may need assistance in finding an alternate provider if illegal billing has occurred.

Test-Taking Strategies Applied

The question contains a qualifying word—FIRST. There may be more than one appropriate response choice, but the order in which they are to occur is critical, with the most immediate or urgent happening first. It is essential that the client report these suspicions to the proper authorities, such as the insurance company, so they can be investigated. Results of this investigation will determine whether a referral to another agency is needed. Two of the response choices have the social worker directly investigating the claims, which is not appropriate.

Knowledge Area

Unit IV—Professional Relationships, Values, and Ethics (Content Area); Professional Values and Ethical Issues (Competency); Legal and/or Ethical Issues Related to the Practice of Social Work, Including Responsibility to Clients/Client Systems, Colleagues, the Profession, and Society (KSA)

14. D

Rationale

Social workers should provide clients with reasonable access to their records. Social workers who are concerned that **clients' access to their records** could cause serious misunderstanding or harm to a client should provide assistance in interpreting the records and consultation with a client regarding the records. Social workers should limit clients' access to their records, or portions of their records, *only in exceptional circumstances when there is compelling evidence that such access would cause serious harm to a client*. Both clients' requests and the rationale for withholding some or all of the record should be documented in clients' files (*NASW Code of Ethics, 2008—1.08 Access to Records*).

In this case scenario, the social worker believes that releasing the record would be harmful based on the client's competency. Thus, denying access at this time and documenting her concerns in the record are appropriate.

The same standard applies whether the client is a former or current client.

Test-Taking Strategies Applied

In practice, social workers often have to make subjective judgments about how the *NASW Code of Ethics* should be applied. On the examination, social workers should adhere to the "facts" provided— not thinking about what they may have done in the past given varying contextual factors. In this case scenario, the actual ability of the client to understand the material in his file is not relevant—the social worker's concern, even if based on inaccurate assumptions, must be the foundation for making the final decision about whether the limiting of the record is ethical. Recalling the material in the *NASW Code of Ethics* about access to records, and the subsequent provision about exceptional circumstances, must be the basis for selecting the correct answer.

Knowledge Area

Unit IV—Professional Relationships, Values, and Ethics (Content Area); Confidentiality (Competency); The Use of Client/Client System Records (KSA)

15. D

Rationale

Although all of the response choices may occur and be useful from a practical perspective, the question asks for the response choice that occurs NEXT according to the principles of **ethical problem solving**.

There are six sequential steps in ethical problem solving—(a) identifying the ethical standards that are being compromised, (b) determining whether an ethical issue or dilemma exists, (c) weighing ethical issues in light of the social work values and principles as defined by the professional code of ethics, (d) suggesting modifications in light of prioritized ethical values and principles, (e) implementing modifications in light of prioritized ethical values and principles, and (f) monitoring for new ethical issues and dilemmas.

As the presence of an ethical dilemma has already been identified (step 2), the social worker should then weigh ethical issues in light of ethical values and principles (step 3).

Test-Taking Strategies Applied

The question contains a qualifying word—NEXT. Its use indicates that the order in which the response choices would occur is critical. Identifying where the social worker is in a process outlined in a case scenario must occur before looking at the answers.

In this case scenario, the existence of an ethical dilemma has been established. The correct answer will be the step that occurs next, as long as it is consistent with the "principles of ethical problem solving."

Knowledge Area

Unit IV—Professional Relationships, Values, and Ethics (Content Area); Professional Values and Ethical Issues (Competency); Techniques to Identify and Resolve Ethical Dilemmas (KSA)

16. C

Rationale

Social workers often may find themselves providing services to **clients who are involuntary** or those who did not choose to receive them, such as the client described in the case scenario. Essential to engagement within the problem-solving process is acknowledging the client's situation and feelings regarding not having complete control over all aspects of life. Building trust is only possible through honesty, including the reasons why the social worker is involved. As the client is mandated into services, there is an inherent lack of trust present. The client may not understand what is happening and how he or she feels about the intervention. Recognizing this ambivalence will help to form a foundation for a connection between a social worker and client—one that can assist the creation of a therapeutic alliance.

Test-Taking Strategies Applied

The question contains a qualifying word—MOST. Although all of the response choices may be important to treatment, there is a unique challenge with providing services to mandated clients; namely, they may not want to be there as they did not voluntarily seek services. Mandated clients may struggle to exert their self-determination, challenging the authority and roles of social workers. They may also be angry about the need for help. Social workers will not be viewed by clients as being understanding without recognizing this situation immediately.

When working with mandated clients, not all information is confidential as asserted by one response choice. Social workers should ensure that involuntary clients know what they have control over and what they do not, as well as what information is confidential and what will be reported to the court or authorizing agency.

Knowledge Area

Unit III—Interventions With Clients/Client Systems (Content Area); Intervention Processes and Techniques (Competency); Methods to Engage and Work With Involuntary Clients/Client Systems (KSA)

17. C

Rationale

Although all of the response choices are important aspects of social work service delivery, this question is seeking a strategy that is useful when working with **clients with multiple problems**. Maslow's hierarchy of needs implies that clients are motivated to meet certain needs. When one need is fulfilled, a client seeks to fulfill the next one, and so on. Maslow saw these needs as comprising a five-stage model with deficiency needs—physiological, safety, social, and esteem—coming before the growth need of self-actualization.

Maslow's hierarchy of needs can be a useful tool for helping decide in what order problems should be addressed. Those related to basic well-being or safety must be considered before those related to socialization and happiness.

Test-Taking Strategies Applied

The question contains a qualifying word—MOST. Although all of the response choices are important to social work practice, social workers must work to prioritize multiple problems when they exist as not all can be addressed simultaneously with clients. None of the answers, except the correct one, provide help or assistance in developing a strategy to select between them.

The correct response choice must directly relate to the presence of multiple problems because this is the focus of the question.

Knowledge Area

Unit II—Assessment (Content Area); Assessment Methods and Techniques (Competency); The Factors and Processes Used in Problem Formulation (KSA)

18. D

Rationale

Pluralism is a belief that people of different social classes, religions, races, and so on, should live together in a society. It also recognizes that these diverse constituents in a society should be able to continue to have their different traditions and interests.

Diversity is representation of those from different social classes, religions, races, and so on. **Equality** is the equal treatment of all, regardless of social class, religion, race, and so on. **Ethnocentrism** is the belief that one's ethnicity is superior to others.

Test-Taking Strategies Applied

The question is seeking a response choice that is a belief or conviction. Diversity is the composition of those from different social classes, religions, races, and so on, but the belief in its value is pluralism.

Selecting the best response is required—though it is not used as a qualifying word. Diversity is when society consists of heterogeneous members, but it is not the best answer. Pluralism represents a belief in the merits of diversity.

Knowledge Area

Unit I—Human Development, Diversity, and Behavior in the Environment (Content Area); Diversity, Social/Economic Justice, and Oppression (Competency); Social and Economic Justice (KSA)

19. D

Rationale

Social workers should protect the **confidentiality of clients during legal proceedings** to the extent permitted by law. When a court of law or other legally authorized body orders social workers to disclose confidential or privileged information without a client's consent and such disclosure could cause harm to a client, social workers should request that the court withdraw the order, limit the order as narrowly as possible, or maintain the records under seal, unavailable for public inspection (*NASW Code of Ethics, 2008—1.07 Privacy and Confidentiality*).

Social workers cannot independently redact information that they believe is harmful as they are legally bound to submit this information. They should use other mechanisms listed to protect client confidentiality to the greatest extent possible.

Test-Taking Strategies Applied

The question contains a qualifying word—EXCEPT. Three of the four response choices are legal and/or ethical mandates of social workers. Social workers should read each answer and ask whether this must be done when court-ordered information is harmful. If so, the response choice can be eliminated as this question is requiring the one answer that is not essential.

Knowledge Area

Unit IV—Professional Relationships, Values, and Ethics (Content Area); Confidentiality (Competency); Legal and/or Ethical Issues Regarding Confidentiality, Including Electronic Information Security (KSA)

20. B

Rationale

Case management has been defined in many ways. However, all models are based on the belief that clients often need assistance in accessing services in today's complex systems, as well as the need to monitor duplication and gaps in treatment and care. Although there may be many federal, state, and local programs available, there are often serious service gaps. A client might have a specific need met in one program and many related needs ignored because of the lack of coordination. Systems are highly complex, fragmented, duplicative, and uncoordinated.

Although the primary goal of social work case management is to optimize client functioning and well-being, it is focused on service provision. Making sure that needs are met is essential—simply identifying them, as indicated by one response choice, is not sufficient.

Case management is not focused on making macro-level changes, though advocacy as part of the process may result in them. Curing emotional or mental dysfunction is not a correct answer based on the person-in-environment (PIE) perspective, which is the basis of social work practice. It views client problems as resulting from role ambiguity or a lack of coping skills that need strengthening, rather than being pathological in nature.

Test-Taking Strategies Applied

The question contains a qualifying word—primary. Unlike in many other questions, the qualifying word is not capitalized. Qualifying words may be capitalized or not, so it is important to read questions carefully. *Primary* means that case management may achieve some of the other goals stated, but its main purpose is the correct response choice.

Knowledge Area

Unit III—Interventions With Clients/Client Systems (Content Area); Intervention Processes and Techniques (Competency); The Components of Case Management (KSA)

21. A

Rationale

Power structure is an overall system of influence with organizations. It captures the way in which power or authority is distributed. Power structures are fluid, with changes in them occurring constantly.

There are distinct types of power—formal and informal. Formal power results from one's position in an organization and the authority associated with that position. Conversely, informal power often stems from the relationships built and respect earned. Although organizational structure determines formal power, other factors, including specialized knowledge, charisma, and persuasive influence, drive informal power.

Those with the most formal power may *not* be the most influential in decision making. There is often resistance within organizations by those with the greatest power when there is any attempt to disrupt the status quo or the current power structures.

Test-Taking Strategies Applied

The question contains a qualifying word—TRUE. It is even capitalized to assist with identifying the distinguishing factor of the correct response from the rest. Each statement must be read carefully and evaluated as to its accuracy. The correct answer is identified through the process of elimination, with each false assertion being excluded.

Knowledge Area

Unit III—Interventions With Clients/Client Systems (Content Area); Use of Collaborative Relationships (Competency); The Relationship Between Formal and Informal Power Structures in the Decision-Making Process (KSA)

22. D

Rationale

Communication between social workers and their clients is interactive and interrelational. Social workers' questions will result in specific responses by clients that, in turn, lead to other inquiries. There are a number of techniques that may be used to assist in this process.

Universalization is the generalization or normalization of behavior. **Clarification** reformulates problems in clients' own words to make sure they are understood. **Interpretation** is the pulling together of behavior patterns to get a new understanding.

Confrontation is calling attention to something, which is what the social worker is doing in the case scenario.

Test-Taking Strategies Applied

This is a recall question that relies on social workers' familiarization with communication strategies or techniques. Although confrontations can be adversarial, they do not have to be. Thus, this answer should *not* be inappropriately eliminated as it is not inherently argumentative.

Knowledge Area

Unit III—Interventions With Clients/Client Systems (Content Area); Intervention Processes and Techniques (Competency); The Principles and Techniques of Interviewing (e.g., Supporting, Clarifying, Focusing, Confronting, Validating, Feedback, Reflecting, Language Differences, Use of Interpreters, Redirecting) (KSA)

23. A

Rationale

Continuum of care is a concept involving an integrated system of care that guides and tracks clients over time through a comprehensive array of services spanning *all levels of intensity of care*. Clients enter treatment at a level appropriate to their needs and then step up to more intense treatment or down to less intense treatment as needed. An effective continuum of care features successful transfer of the client between levels of care, similar treatment philosophy across levels of care, and efficient transfer of client records. Levels in a continuum of care may vary, but can include early intervention services, outpatient services, intensive outpatient/partial hospitalization services, residential/inpatient services, and medically managed intensive inpatient services.

Test-Taking Strategies Applied

The question contains a qualifying word—MOST. Although the existence of a continuum of care can affect quality and has been found to be effective as a method to increase or decrease service utilization (thereby being efficient), it is inherently based on matching the client's needs with service intensity.

Knowledge Area

Unit II—Assessment (Content Area); Assessment Methods and Techniques (Competency); Placement Options Based on Assessed Level of Care (KSA)

24. B

Rationale

Dual or multiple relationships occur when social workers relate to clients in more than one relationship, whether professional, social, or business. Dual or multiple relationships can occur simultaneously or consecutively. Social workers should be alert to and avoid conflicts of interest that interfere with the exercise of professional discretion and impartial judgment. Social workers should inform clients when a real or potential conflict of interest arises and take reasonable steps to resolve the issue in a manner that makes clients' interests primary and protects clients' interests to the greatest extent possible. In some cases, protecting clients' interests may require termination of the professional relationship with proper referral of clients. However, the procedures for termination are not the primary concern as resolution of the case scenario may be resolved via an alternative method (such as transferring to another social worker).

Strict adherence to confidentiality standards and understanding the power differentials between a social worker and client are critical in the delivery of all services. Learning that the client is the sister of a best friend does not increase their importance.

Test-Taking Strategies Applied

The question contains a qualifying word—primary—though it is not capitalized. The relationship between the client and the social worker's best friend is the problem at hand. This is a conflict of interest and needs to be addressed, though it is unclear if termination is the most appropriate option. Discussion with the client must occur. If termination is warranted, learning about and adhering to the procedures for termination is not likely to be problematic.

Knowledge Area

Unit IV—Professional Relationships, Values, and Ethics (Content Area); Professional Values and Ethical Issues (Competency); Ethical Issues Related to Dual Relationships (KSA)

25. B

Rationale

Social workers respect and promote the right of clients to **self-determination** and assist clients in their efforts to identify and clarify their goals. Social workers may limit clients' right to self-determination when, in a social workers' professional judgment, clients' actions or potential actions pose a serious, foreseeable, and imminent risk to themselves or others. Client self-determination may not be limited based on a professional's thought that other choices are better.

In situations where clients are deemed dangerous to themselves or others because of their mental status, they can be made to go into psychiatric hospitals or other treatment facilities against their will. This process is called involuntary commitment and every state has a law for it, although those laws are often not well known. Clients cannot be held in inpatient settings against their will if they are not a danger to self or others, even when outpatient alternatives are not available.

In instances when clients are receiving services involuntarily, such as through involuntary commitment, social workers should provide information about services and the extent of clients' rights to refuse these services.

Test-Taking Strategies Applied

This is a recall question that relies on social workers understanding the legal issues regarding clients' rights to self-determination and their limits. It is essential for social workers to understand clients' rights to refuse services and when they can be mandated. This information must also be transmitted to clients so that they can make informed choices.

Knowledge Area

Unit IV—Professional Relationships, Values, and Ethics (Content Area); Professional Values and Ethical Issues (Competency); The Client/Client System's Right to Refuse Services (e.g., Medication, Medical Treatment, Counseling, Placement, etc.) (KSA)

26. D

Rationale

Separation anxiety occurs when babies begin to understand that they are a separate person from their primary caregiver but still have not mastered the concept of object permanence—the idea that something still exists when it is not seen or heard. Thus, when babies are separated from their primary caregivers, they do not understand that their caregivers will return. Because babies do not have a concept of time, they fear that the departure of their parents is permanent. Separation anxiety resolves as children develop a sense of memory. They can keep an image of their parents in mind when the parents are gone and can recall that, in the past, the parents returned.

Separation anxiety is manifested by fussing and crying when a parent leaves the room. Some children scream and have tantrums, refuse to leave their parents' side, and/or have nighttime awakenings.

Separation anxiety is a typical stage of development and typically begins at about 6 to 8 months and peaks in intensity by about 18 months.

Test-Taking Strategies Applied

The question contains a qualifying word—OFTEN. Its use acknowledges that child development is individualized and children can enter stages at varying ages. However, the typical age at which separation begins is 6 to 8 months. It is stronger in intensity between 14 and 18 months—which is closer to another response choice, but not the correct one. This question is asking about when it usually starts—not when it is strongest.

Knowledge Area

Unit I—Human Development, Diversity, and Behavior in the Environment (Content Area); Human Growth and Development (Competency); The Principles of Attachment and Bonding (KSA)

27. B

Rationale

Denial is the most common defense mechanism and is an inability to acknowledge the significance or implications of a thought, feeling, wish, or behavior, such as the client's drinking being a problem, as evidenced by his arrests.

Rationalization is a cognitive distortion to make an event or an impulse less threatening. It makes this event or impulse more acceptable. **Projection** involves individuals attributing their own thoughts, feelings, and motives to others. Thoughts most commonly projected are the ones that would cause guilt. **Sublimation** is when a maladaptive feeling or behavior is diverted into a socially acceptable, adaptive one (i.e., someone with aggression problems becoming a boxer).

Test-Taking Strategies Applied

The question contains a qualifying word—MOST. It is possible that the client could be using rationalization to explain his arrests by attributing them to factors other than drinking. However, there are no other reasons generated by the client that are included in the case scenario. Thus, the client is MOST likely in denial about the existence of a substance use problem.

Knowledge Area

Unit I—Human Development, Diversity, and Behavior in the Environment (Content Area); Human Behavior in the Social Environment (Competency); Psychological Defense Mechanisms and Their Effects on Behavior and Relationships (KSA)

28. C

Rationale

There are many signs of substance abuse, including, but not limited to:

- *Secrecy*: hiding the amount of drugs or alcohol consumed
- *Changing appearance*: deterioration in hygiene or physical appearance—lack of showering, slovenly appearance, unclean clothes
- *Neglecting other interests/activities*: spending less time on activities that used to be important (hanging out with family and friends, exercising, pursuing hobbies, or other interests)

Although a family history of addiction is a risk factor for substance abuse, it is not a sign or result of this abuse.

Test-Taking Strategies Applied

This question requires careful reading because all response choices are related to substance abuse. However, a family history of abuse is not a sign of—but rather a risk factor for—substance abuse. A family history of addiction can dramatically increase one's predisposition to substance abuse. Signs are factors that may result from abuse of substances, but they do not lead to a greater likelihood of having this problem.

Knowledge Area

Unit II—Assessment (Content Area); Assessment Methods and Techniques (Competency); The Indicators of Addiction and Substance Abuse (KSA)

29. D

Rationale

Social workers often work together with those from various professions. This is known as an **interdisciplinary approach**. In this case scenario, the client's changes appear to coincide with a medical diagnosis and the prescribing of a new medication. The client may be experiencing symptoms of this physical disorder or side effects of the medication that he is taking. The social worker must rule out the medical etiology of these feelings and behaviors before looking for other causes or intervening.

Test-Taking Strategies Applied

The question contains a qualifying word—FIRST. There may be more than one appropriate response choice, but the order in which they are to occur is critical, with the most immediate or urgent happening first. Attention to health and safety are always primary. Although the client reports being depressed, there is no indication of suicide risk. In fact, his desire to develop new hobbies indicates he is thinking about the future. The social worker must collaborate with the client's physician because his signs may be tied to his medical status or the medication that he has been prescribed—both of which are within the scope of practice of the physician.

Knowledge Area

Unit III—Interventions With Clients/Client Systems (Content Area); Use of Collaborative Relationships (Competency); The Process of Interdisciplinary and Intradisciplinary Team Collaboration (KSA)

30. B

Rationale

Piaget's four stages of **cognitive development** are:

- Sensorimotor—birth through 24 months
- Preoperational—toddlerhood (2 years) through early childhood (age 7)
- Concrete operational—ages 7 to 11
- Formal operational—age 11 through adulthood

Piaget acknowledged that some children may pass through the stages at different ages than the averages noted, and that some children may show characteristics of more than one stage at a given time. But he insisted that cognitive development always follows this sequence, that stages cannot be skipped, and that each stage is marked by new intellectual abilities and a more complex understanding of the world.

The concrete operational stage is characterized by the beginnings of abstract thoughts. However, cause-and-effect relationships and rules are very important. Rules of logic are understood so deviations or exceptions are often viewed negatively.

Test-Taking Strategies Applied

The question contains a qualifying word—MOST. While the child may be at another cognitive stage, his behavior is clearly indicative of the concrete operational stage. In addition, the age of the child is provided as an additional clue to the correct response choice because most children pass through this stage from ages 7 to 11.

Knowledge Area

Unit I—Human Development, Diversity, and Behavior in the Environment (Content Area); Human Growth and Development (Competency); Theories of Human Development Throughout the Lifespan (e.g., Physical, Social, Emotional, Cognitive, Behavioral) (KSA)

31. D

Rationale

Multiculturalism is an acknowledgment that people are culturally diverse and multifaceted. It is more of a perspective or mind-set as opposed to a single practice. Social workers should view clients as the "experts" in defining their own cultural experiences. Social workers must acknowledge that there is more difference within than between cultural groups. Multiculturalism is a continual process with clients' own cultures changing as they interact with and are influenced by others.

Test-Taking Strategies Applied

The question contains a qualifying word—BEST. While some of the response choices may be important when working with diverse cultural groups, they are not correct answers as they represent discrete actions or only address one aspect of multiculturalism. For example, ensuring documents are translated into other languages is necessary, but not sufficient for multicultural practice. Without the proper view of clients' culture, social workers cannot ensure that multiculturalism influences all aspects of their practice.

Knowledge Area

Unit I—Human Development, Diversity, and Behavior in the Environment (Content Area); Diversity, Social/Economic Justice, and Oppression (Competency); The Principles of Culturally Competent Social Work Practice (KSA)

32. C

Rationale

Strengths-based generalist practice requires social workers to recognize the power they bring to helping relationships and to engage clients in an open discussion of the various sources of power in their relationships. Acknowledging the inherent **power differential between social workers and their clients** is the first step in shifting the balance of power to clients. *Although they rarely mention it, clients are acutely aware of the power differential between themselves and their social workers.* Opening up the topic for discussion is in itself empowering. It gives social workers and clients an opportunity to evaluate the resources available to address clients' areas of concern. Clients are given a voice in defining the resources and determining how they will be used.

Social workers inherently have three types of power: **expert**, derived from access to and command of specialized knowledge; **referent**, derived from their interpersonal skills; and **legitimate**, derived from their sanctioned position. Thus, they derive power from their expertise, interpersonal skills, and their control of resources needed by clients. Social work effectiveness is predicated on the reduction of the power differential between social workers and their clients, specifically on increasing clients' power resources.

Test-Taking Strategies Applied

The question contains a qualifying word—NOT—that requires social workers to select the response choice that is incorrect about power in the therapeutic relationship. When NOT is used as a qualifying word, it is often helpful to remove it from the question and eliminate the three response choices that *are* correct. This approach will leave the one response choice that is NOT accurate.

Knowledge Area

Unit IV—Professional Relationships, Values, and Ethics (Content Area); Professional Development and Use of Self (Competency); The Components of the Social Worker–Client/Client System Relationship (KSA)

33. C

Rationale

According to the *NASW Code of Ethics*, social workers who **refer clients to other professionals** should take appropriate steps to facilitate an orderly transfer of responsibility. Social workers who refer clients to other professionals should disclose, with clients' consent, all pertinent information to the new service providers.

In the case scenario, it is unclear as to whether the social worker referred the client to the psychologist, but his need for "pertinent information" is known. By providing information directly to the client, the social worker allows the client to decide what he would like to share with the psychologist or not share. The *NASW Code of Ethics* states that social workers should provide clients with reasonable access to their records unless there are concerns that this information would be harmful, which is not the situation presented in the case scenario.

The other response choices are incorrect. Sharing information with other professionals is not prohibited. The entire file should not be sent to the psychologist as only pertinent information is needed and the file may contain confidential material that does not need to be shared. If the social worker waits until the psychologist requests the information, it may be too late to be useful for the assessment.

Providing the information to the client empowers him and allows him to make decisions with the psychologist about what is "pertinent."

Test-Taking Strategies Applied

The question requires the social worker to "best address this request ethically." Whenever ethical mandates of social workers are the foci of questions, the *NASW Code of Ethics* must be recalled. The answer that most closely resembles the wording of the *Code* should be selected.

Knowledge Area

Unit IV—Professional Relationships, Values, and Ethics (Content Area); Confidentiality (Competency); Legal and/or Ethical Issues Regarding Confidentiality, Including Electronic Information Security (KSA)

34. A

Rationale

Social workers often use collateral sources—family, friends, other agencies, physicians, and so on—as informants when collecting information to effectively treat clients. These sources can provide vital information because other professionals or agencies may have treated clients in the past. Family members and friends may also provide important information about the length or severity of issues or problems. It may also provide contextual or background information that a client may not know.

Collateral information is often used when the credibility and validity of information obtained from a client or others are questionable.

When an account by a collateral informant agrees with information gathered from a client, it enhances the trustworthiness of the data collected. Using multiple information sources (or triangulation) is an excellent method for social workers to have accurate accounts upon which to make assessments or base interventions.

With clients' consent, it may be helpful to elicit natural supports, such as family and friends, to assist in resolving problems, but this action is not a justification for *obtaining collateral information*. Collateral information is used to enhance assessment, whereas building clients' support networks is an intervention.

Test-Taking Strategies Applied

The question contains a qualifying word—NOT—that requires social workers to select the response choice that is not a reason to obtain collateral information. When NOT is used as a qualifying word, it is often helpful to remove it from the question and eliminate the three response choices that *are* reasons for gathering information from collateral sources. This approach will leave the one response choice that is NOT a reason.

Knowledge Area

Unit II—Assessment (Content Area); Assessment Methods and Techniques (Competency); Methods of Involving Clients/Client Systems in Problem Identification (e.g., Gathering Collateral Information) (KSA)

35. C

Rationale

The question calls for the social worker to "MOST effectively help this client deal with her anger." In order to do so, she needs to learn strategies to express her positive and negative feelings and to stand up for herself in ways that will not alienate her parents.

Assertiveness training typically begins with clients thinking about areas in their lives in which they have difficulty asserting themselves. The next stage usually involves role plays designed to help clients practice clearer and more direct forms of communicating with others. Feedback is provided to improve responses, and the role play is repeated. Assertiveness training promotes the use of "I" statements as a way to help clients express their feelings.

Determining the frequency and severity of the client's self-destructive actions will not help her deal with her anger. The second sentence in the case scenario is important as she is not able to effectively communicate her feelings. Thus, her anger will continue until communication improves. Assessing the parent's feelings about her behavior does not address the root of the problem. The client is the adolescent, so meeting with the family is not appropriate. Conflict resolution strategies are also not possible without the adolescent being able to express her views effectively.

Test-Taking Strategies Applied

The question contains a qualifying word—MOST. Although the social worker may engage in some of the actions listed, the correct response choice is the most salient intervention for addressing the problem—the adolescent's inability to tell her parents her feelings.

Knowledge Area

Unit III—Interventions With Clients/Client Systems (Content Area); Intervention Processes and Techniques (Competency); Assertiveness Training (KSA)

36. B

Rationale

The Substance-Related and Addictive Disorders chapter in the *DSM-5* includes Gambling Disorder as the sole condition in a new category on behavioral addictions. *DSM-IV-TR* listed Pathological Gambling under the Impulse-Control Disorders Not Elsewhere Classified. Gambling Disorder in this chapter reflects research findings that Gambling Disorder is similar to Substance-Related Disorders in clinical expression, brain origin, comorbidity, physiology, and treatment.

While Gambling Disorder is the only addictive disorder included in the *DSM-5* as a diagnosable condition, Internet Gaming Disorder is included in Section III of the *DSM-5*. Disorders listed there require further research before their consideration as formal disorders. This condition is included to reflect the scientific literature on persistent and recurrent use of Internet games, and a preoccupation with them, appearing to result in clinically significant impairment or distress.

Although there is a consensus on the identification of Gambling Disorder as a behavioral addiction, there is no agreement on whether other excessive behaviors with mixed impulsive and compulsive features (such as compulsive buying and hypersexuality) are related to Substance Use Disorders and should, therefore, be considered as behavioral addictions.

Test-Taking Strategies Applied

This is a recall question that relies on social workers understanding addictive disorders. Although it is clear that excessive buying, sexual activity, and gaming can cause clinical distress, Gambling Disorder is the only behavioral addiction recognized in the *DSM-5*. Further research is needed to clinically link the others to substance-related disorders as opposed to obsessive–compulsive and impulse control issues.

Knowledge Area

Unit II—Assessment (Content Area); Assessment Methods and Techniques (Competency); The Diagnostic and Statistical Manual of the American Psychiatric Association (KSA)

37. B

Rationale

The "sandwich generation" describes those who find themselves squeezed between **caregiving** for younger loved ones such as children and their older parents or other family members. Clients who are part of the sandwich generation—that is, those who have a living parent age 65 or older and are either raising a child under age 18 or supporting a grown child—are pulled in many directions. Not only do they provide care and financial assistance to their parents and their children, but caregivers are pillars of emotional support as well. Life in the sandwich generation is stressful and requires managing competing obligations.

Test-Taking Strategies Applied

This is a recall question that relies on social workers knowing about caregiving, including its effects. Providing care can have harmful physical, mental, and emotional consequences for the caregiver. Social workers must be aware of and mitigate these negative outcomes. Increasing appropriate mental health services and medical care for family caregivers is important. Caregiver education, respite, and financial assistance are essential.

Knowledge Area

Unit III—Interventions With Clients/Client Systems (Content Area); Indicators and Effects of Crisis and Change (Competency); The Impact of Caregiving on Families (KSA)

38. C

Rationale

One of the ways that social workers provide information to clients is through **psychoeducation**. The client has indicated a gap in knowledge by not knowing what to do. The social worker can provide the client with information necessary so that the client can act with enhanced confidence. This information will provide the client with a clearer understanding of the problem, as well as strategies for addressing it. The core psychoeducational principle is that education has a role in emotional and behavioral change.

The other response choices either do not "assist" the client—which is the focus of the question—or address the problem in the best manner, because they do not provide for the client to learn additional skills.

Test-Taking Strategies Applied

The question contains a qualifying word—BEST. Although having respite may be useful for a new mother, or learning about the client's past child-care experiences can shed light on her distress, it is most useful to address the root cause of the problem. The client states that she "does not know what to do," which indicates a lack of knowledge. *When words are in quotation marks in questions, they should be considered carefully as they are included for a reason.* They usually relate directly to the correct answer and distinguish it from the other response choices.

Knowledge Area

Unit III—Interventions With Clients/Client Systems (Content Area); Intervention Processes and Techniques (Competency); Psychoeducation Methods (e.g., Acknowledging, Supporting, Normalizing) (KSA)

39. D

Rationale

Social work scholars distinguish spirituality from religion. **Spirituality** has been described as the basic essence of the individual, as well as how an individual finds meaning and purpose through relationships with self, others, and a higher power. Spirituality encompasses an experience of meaning, purpose, and fulfillment in relationship with self, others, and a higher being that is innate in all human beings. Although spirituality is generally seen as referring to human experiences that transcend the self, religion is generally described in terms of formal institutions for spiritual beliefs and practices. Accordingly, **religion** has been defined as a communal setting through which beliefs are organized and spirituality is practiced. Thus, religion is encompassed within spirituality, but spirituality is viewed as broader than religion. Spirituality is not connected to any particular theology and is not equivalent with religion. Therefore, spirituality can be expressed in any particular religious context.

Religion is not an experience, but rather settings in which spirituality and associated traditions can be practiced, making the last response choice NOT true of religion.

Test-Taking Strategies Applied

The question contains a qualifying word—NOT—that requires social workers to select the response choice that is not true regarding spirituality and religion. It is critical to be able to tease out what is being stated about spirituality and religion in each of the response choices and weigh its accuracy. The response choice with factual inaccuracies related to religion and spirituality is correct.

Knowledge Area

Unit I—Human Development, Diversity, and Behavior in the Environment (Content Area); Human Growth and Development (Competency); Theories of Spiritual Development Throughout the Lifespan (KSA)

40. C

Rationale

An organization is a group of people who work together to achieve a common goal. In order to work together efficiently, the group must find the best way to organize the work that needs to be done in order to meet the goals of the organization. **Organizational structure** defines how tasks are divided, grouped, and coordinated in organizations. Every organization has a structure that clarifies the roles that organizational members perform, so that all understand their responsibilities to the group. Based on the organizational structure, members know what to do and who to report to. The structure also dictates the amount of control organizational members have regarding their jobs in the organization.

Organizations use diagrams called **organizational charts** that display the structures of organizations and also show the relationships between organizational members and the ranks of all the positions in the organization.

Test-Taking Strategies Applied

The question contains a qualifying word—MOST. It is possible that a social worker may gain some insight into processes from an organizational chart, but it is most useful in understanding structure. A flow chart, not an organizational chart, is preferred for outlining steps in a process.

Knowledge Area

Unit II—Assessment (Content Area); Assessment Methods and Techniques (Competency); Methods to Assess the Client's/Client

System's Strengths, Resources, and Challenges (e.g., Individual, Family, Group, Organization, Community) (KSA)

41. D

Rationale

Alzheimer's disease and **dementia** are mistakenly used interchangeably at times, but there is a distinct difference. Dementia refers to a set of symptoms, not the disease itself. These symptoms might include language difficulty, loss of recent memory, or poor judgment. In other words, when a client is said to have dementia, he or she is exhibiting certain symptoms. With a thorough screening including blood tests (to rule out other causes of dementia such as vitamin deficiency), a mental status evaluation, neuropsychological testing, and sometimes a brain scan, doctors can accurately diagnose the cause of the dementia symptoms in most cases. However, Alzheimer's can be diagnosed with complete accuracy only after death, using a microscopic examination of brain tissue that checks for plaques and tangles.

Although Alzheimer's disease accounts for most cases of dementia, there are other disorders that cause dementia. In the early stages of diseases, there usually are some clear differences between the diseases. As they advance, however, more parts of the brain become affected and the differences between one cause of dementia and another are subtle.

Test-Taking Strategies Applied

The question contains a qualifying word—BEST. Although parts of the incorrect response choices may be true, the correct answer is the only one that accurately describes the relationship between Alzheimer's disease and dementia.

Knowledge Area

Unit I—Human Development, Diversity, and Behavior in the Environment (Content Area); Human Growth and Development (Competency); The Indicators of Normal and Abnormal Physical, Cognitive, Emotional, and Sexual Development Throughout the Lifespan (KSA)

42. D

Rationale

Age of consent means the age at which an individual can have sexual intercourse with whomever he or she wishes as long as that person is consenting and is the same age or older. The age of consent varies between 16 and 18 years old, depending upon the state. Most, but not all, have an age of consent of 16 years old.

Until recently, the statutory rape laws applied only to girls, not to boys; sexual intercourse with an underage boy was not legally statutory rape. Age of consent is culturally based, and many other countries have younger ages. For example, it is 13 years old in South Korea and Japan and, until recently, Spain. It is 14 years old in Austria, Germany, Italy, and Portugal, and 15 years old in Denmark, France, and Sweden.

Test-Taking Strategies Applied

This is a recall question that relies on social workers knowing about minors and self-determination. They should understand that informed consent is really not an "on/off" process that is dictated by age. However, there are laws that determine at what age individuals must be to legally give consent for sexual intercourse.

Knowledge Area

Unit IV—Professional Relationships, Values, and Ethics (Content Area); Professional Values and Ethical Issues (Competency); Client/Client System Competence and Self-Determination (e.g., Financial Decisions, Treatment Decisions, Emancipation, Age of Consent, Permanency Planning) (KSA)

43. C

Rationale

Empathy can be defined as the act of perceiving, understanding, experiencing, and responding to the emotional state and ideas of a client. The act of empathy reflects the social work core value of dignity and worth of the person. It is based on respecting clients' unique situations, strengths, weaknesses, and what is important to them about their presenting issues and problems.

The question requires the identification of the least effective action to show or demonstrate empathy to clients. Empathetic communication must be nonjudgmental, accepting, and genuine. Social workers must view clients as experts in their own life circumstances and respect them by listening to and validating their opinions.

Although it is essential for clients to understand the roles of social workers in the helping process, this knowledge is not directly related to demonstrating empathy with clients. It is not an empathetic communication method like the other response choices and is, therefore, the least likely to show clients that social workers are empathetic.

Test-Taking Strategies Applied

The question contains a qualifying word—LEAST. Although all of the response choices may relate to empathetic communication, the response choice that relates to the demonstration of empathy in the most minimal way must be selected. The other answers view the client as the expert with the social worker listening, not passing judgment, and validating. The correct answer does not directly relate to the client's feelings—but rather providing factual information about the social worker's role.

Knowledge Area

Unit IV—Professional Relationships, Values, and Ethics (Content Area); Professional Values and Ethical Issues (Competency); The Concept of Acceptance and Empathy in the Social Worker–Client/Client System Relationship (KSA)

44. B

Rationale

The U.S. Environmental Protection Agency's (EPA) definition of **environmental justice** establishes it as a social justice issue: Environmental justice is the fair treatment and meaningful involvement of all people regardless of race, color, sex, national origin, or income with respect to the development, implementation, and enforcement of environmental laws, regulations, and policies.

Environmental destruction and devastation disproportionately impact disadvantaged and marginalized groups. Environmental pollution is greater in minority and low-income communities. Thus, minority and poor communities bear the burden of environmental problems that are forced upon them by decision makers and more empowered communities that subscribe to the notion of "not in my back yard."

Although forming multidisciplinary partnerships and building the scholarly knowledge base are important steps toward achieving environmental justice, they are not the reasons that social workers should be concerned with this issue. Being recognized as a profession that is nondiscriminatory by closing the gap between social and environmental justice concerns is also not the primary concern.

Social workers should be concerned with client welfare and the disproportionate treatment of those without power, which is the basis of the correct answer.

Test-Taking Strategies Applied

The question contains a qualifying word—PRIMARY—that indicates that social workers may be concerned with environmental justice for more than one of the reasons stated, but the main purpose must be selected from the rest. The incorrect answers do not directly relate to environmental justice as it affects clients—instead, they focus on its importance to the profession and/or how social workers can assist. The benefit to clients is always the primary concern of social workers.

Knowledge Area

Unit I—Human Development, Diversity, and Behavior in the Environment (Content Area); Diversity, Social/Economic Justice, and Oppression (Competency); Social and Economic Justice (KSA)

45. B

Rationale

When leading groups, social workers have many facilitating tasks. At the beginning of the **group process**, it is important for group members to understand group purposes, their roles and those of social workers, and organizational logistics and guidelines. Groups should also set plans. Although members are likely to be distant or removed until they have time to develop relationships, social workers should elicit input from group members so that they can feel "ownership" of the process. The ability of group members to make key decisions about "rules" will make it more likely that those rules will be followed in the future. It also gives members an opportunity to begin to interact with one another.

Test-Taking Strategies Applied

Groups optimally function when they are the helping agent and responsible for themselves. All of the response choices, except the correct one, have the social worker making decisions or setting the rules. Although social workers will need to be more active in the beginning phase of group development, they should elicit input whenever possible from group members and only intervene when necessary to maximize effectiveness.

Knowledge Area

Unit I—Human Development, Diversity, and Behavior in the Environment (Content Area); Human Behavior in the Social Environment (Competency); Theories of Group Development and Functioning (KSA)

46. D

Rationale

Psychological or emotional abuse is sustained, repetitive, and inappropriate behavior aimed at threatening, isolating, discrediting, belittling, teasing, humiliating, bullying, confusing, and/or ignoring. Psychological or emotional abuse can be seen in constant criticism, belittling, teasing, ignoring or withholding of praise or affection, and placing excessive or unreasonable demands, including expectations above what is appropriate.

It can impact intelligence, memory, recognition, perception, attention, imagination, and moral development. Individuals who have been psychologically abused are likely to be fearful, withdrawn, and/or resentful, distressed, and despairing. They are likely to feel unloved, worthless, and unwanted, or only valued in meeting another's needs. Those who are victims of psychological or emotional abuse often avoid eye contact and experience deep loneliness, anxiety, and/or despair; have a flat and superficial way of relating, with little empathy toward others; have a lowered capacity to engage appropriately with others; engage in bullying, disruptive, or aggressive behaviors toward others; and/or engage in self-harming and/or self-destructive behaviors (i.e., cutting, physical aggression, reckless behavior showing a disregard for self and safety, drug taking).

Test-Taking Strategies Applied

The question contains a qualifying word—EXCEPT. Three of the four response choices are signs of emotional abuse. The case scenario states that the child is not being sexually or physically abused. Unexplained physical markings are associated with these types of abuse, not emotional abuse.

Knowledge Area

Unit II—Assessment (Content Area); Concepts of Abuse and Neglect (Competency); The Effects of Physical, Sexual, and Psychological Abuse on Individuals, Families, Groups, Organizations, and Communities (KSA)

47. C

Rationale

Discharge planning is a critical social work function. It involves linking clients with vital resources that are outside of the inpatient setting to ensure continuity of care or the provision of follow-up services. Often, discharge planning is an interdisciplinary process and includes occupational therapy, speech therapy, nursing, and so on. The goal of discharge planning is improving the general welfare and well-being of clients.

Discharge planning must be tailored for different needs of clients and be comprehensive. It must create a system that is continuous and coordinated. Discharge plans must be practical and realistic and maximize available community resources for the benefit of the client.

Although there is not a standard format for discharge plans, they should contain:

- Reasons for care and services provided while in the care of discharge entity/agency

- Information related to client/achievement of treatment goals/ outcomes
- Primary or significant problems/issues identified during treatment stay
- Assessment of client level of functioning/progress made
- Reason for discharge
- Service needs at discharge
- Referrals provided for ongoing treatment

Test-Taking Strategies Applied

The question contains a qualifying word—NOT—that requires social workers to select a response choice which does not need to be in a discharge plan. Although discharge plans may contain the type of ongoing treatment needed (including the agencies to provide it if known), it will not typically include a listing of all agencies that provide ongoing treatment. Such a listing would not be helpful to clients because it places the responsibility to see if there are openings and make appointments on them. Social workers should make follow-up appointments with ongoing treatment providers for clients prior to their discharge.

Knowledge Area

Unit III—Interventions With Clients/Client Systems (Content Area); Intervention Processes and Techniques (Competency); Discharge, Aftercare, and Follow-Up Planning (KSA)

48. B

Rationale

Clients may experience a **lack of readiness to participate in the intervention process** and engage in resistant behaviors. These can include not keeping appointments, withholding information, false promising, and so on.

However, social workers should not automatically assume these behaviors result from resistance or a lack of commitment to services. In this case scenario, the client is actively reaching out to indicate the inability to attend appointments, which demonstrates engagement. The client has many demands on her time that may be the cause of her poor attendance. The incorrect answers are punitive or inappropriately speculate that she is not motivated. At the next meeting, the social worker must discuss the client's absences with her and brainstorm as to whether her needs can be met in a more accessible manner.

Test-Taking Strategies Applied

Answers must be assessed with the understanding that the correct one is that which most effectively helps the client. The incorrect answers make assumptions about the client's behavior without her input. Several are also punitive, such as charging fees and discontinuing services. Neither of these actions helps the client get the services needed to address the stress imposed by caring for her parents.

Knowledge Area

Unit II—Assessment (Content Area); Assessment Methods and Techniques (Competency); Methods to Assess Motivation, Resistance, and Readiness to Change (KSA)

49. D

Rationale

Human trafficking has been used as an umbrella term for activities involved when someone obtains or holds a person in compelled service. Individuals may be trafficking victims regardless of whether they once consented, participated in a crime as a direct result of being trafficked, were transported into the exploitative situation, or were simply born into a state of servitude. Major forms of human trafficking include forced labor, sex trafficking, bonded labor, involuntary domestic servitude, forced child labor, child soldiers, and so on.

Once it is suspected that a client is a victim of human trafficking, the client should be helped to find a safe place to go immediately. In some ways, treatment is similar to working with a victim of domestic violence. Both types of victims are in grave danger.

Test-Taking Strategies Applied

The question contains a qualifying word—FIRST. There may be more than one appropriate response choice, but the order in which they are to occur is critical, with the most immediate or urgent happening first. Maslow's hierarchy of needs can be a useful tool for helping to decide in what order problems should be addressed. Those related to safety of the client must be considered before finding out what led to the exploitation and addressing the emotional consequences. Although learning whether there are other victims may be important to assisting them, the social worker must first make sure that the client is safe.

Knowledge Area

Unit II—Assessment (Content Area); Concepts of Abuse and Neglect (Competency); The Indicators, Dynamics, and Impact of Exploitation Across the Lifespan (e.g., Financial, Immigration Status, Sexual Trafficking) (KSA)

50. A

Rationale

Psychosis is when a client has a break from reality and often involves seeing, hearing, and believing things that are not real. Psychosis is not an illness, but a symptom. A psychotic episode can be the result of a mental or physical illness, substance use, trauma, or extreme stress. Symptoms of a psychotic episode can include incoherent speech and disorganized behavior, such as unpredictable anger. Psychosis typically involves **hallucinations** (seeing, hearing, or physically feeling things that are not actually there) or **delusions** (strong beliefs that are unlikely to be true and may seem irrational to others).

Once a diagnosis is made, prescription of a medication is usually needed to control the hallucinations or delusions. Group therapy, behavior management, and individual psychotherapy can be helpful as augmentative treatments, but psychopharmacology is most effective.

Test-Taking Strategies Applied

The question contains a qualifying word—MOST. Although all of the response choices may be helpful for clients who are psychotic, medications reduce psychotic symptoms most effectively and appropriately. However, antipsychotic drugs do not cure mental illnesses that cause psychosis and cannot ensure that there will be no further psychotic episodes.

Knowledge Area

Unit II—Assessment (Content Area); Biopsychosocial History and Collateral Data (Competency); The Indicators of Mental and Emotional Illness Throughout the Lifespan (KSA)

51. B

Rationale

Social workers often rely on the expertise of others to assist in determining the causes of client problems. For example, social workers must always first determine if client actions are due to a medical or substance use issue before attributing them to psychological factors.

Social workers should be knowledgeable about the scopes of practice of professionals in other disciplines (e.g., medicine, psychology), in addition to understanding what their own education, training, experience, and laws/regulations allow them to do. Social workers must **refer clients to other professionals** when the other professionals' specialized knowledge or expertise is needed to fully evaluate clients. Social workers must refer to competent providers—those educated, trained, and certified/licensed to perform the evaluations needed.

In this case scenario, there is no indication of developmental delays and it is not appropriate to meet with the daughter because the mother is the client. Although bedwetting can be tied to sexual abuse, there are no other signs of maltreatment. Bedwetting is most often tied to medical or physiological problems and an evaluation by a doctor is needed to make an initial assessment.

Test-Taking Strategies Applied

The question contains a qualifying word—FIRST. A medical evaluation is a critical part of assessing what is causing the bedwetting. If it has no medical etiology, other actions, including possibly one or more of those listed, may be taken to determine the cause. It is essential to initially rule out biological roots, which can only be done by a physician.

Knowledge Area

Unit III—Interventions With Clients/Client Systems (Content Area); Use of Collaborative Relationships (Competency); Consultation Approaches (e.g., Referrals to Specialists) (KSA)

52. A

Rationale

Although caregiving is at the heart of family functioning, the dynamics of families can be greatly altered when family members experience **illness or disability**. For example, when a primary family caregiver becomes ill or disabled, family roles must shift to redistribute the tasks he or she is unable to perform. This redistribution includes both instrumental and emotional tasks, as the family may face a loss of both financial and emotional support that was provided by the primary family caregiver.

Test-Taking Strategies Applied

The question requires the correct answer to be distinguished from the incorrect ones based on the use of "a systems approach." Systems theory states that an entire system changes when one part of it does. In this case scenario, the medical crisis of the client's wife will disrupt the steady state (homeostasis) within the family and require new roles to be undertaken by others in the family, at least temporarily.

Knowledge Area

Unit II—Assessment (Content Area); Biopsychosocial History and Collateral Data (Competency); Biopsychosocial Responses to Illness and Disability (KSA)

53. B

Rationale

Drug and alcohol withdrawal can result in physical and emotional effects. Some drugs produce significant physical withdrawal (alcohol, opiates, and tranquilizers). Some drugs produce little physical withdrawal but more emotional withdrawal (cocaine, marijuana, and ecstasy). Every client's physical withdrawal is different. Some experience little physical withdrawal and more emotional withdrawal.

Alcohol and tranquilizers produce the most dangerous physical withdrawal. Suddenly stopping alcohol or tranquilizers can lead to seizures, strokes, or heart attacks. A medically supervised detox can minimize withdrawal symptoms and reduce the risk of dangerous complications. Some of the dangerous symptoms of alcohol and tranquilizer withdrawal are grand mal seizures, heart attacks, strokes, and hallucinations.

Test-Taking Strategies Applied

Although the question does not explicitly state that Maslow's hierarchy of needs should be used, it requires that the correct answer is one "to meet his (the client's) needs." Maslow's hierarchy of needs is a useful tool for helping decide in what order actions should be taken. With regard to substance use, addressing the social-emotional and other effects of addiction, along with constructing a relapse prevention plan, are done after dealing with the immediate health needs associated with withdrawal.

Knowledge Area

Unit I—Human Development, Diversity, and Behavior in the Environment (Content Area); Human Behavior in the Social Environment (Competency); Addiction Theories and Concepts (KSA)

54. A

Rationale

There are patterns of behavior or **family roles** that exist in all families. However, in those that have been affected by addiction, the roles might seem like they are cast in concrete. They are not conscious choices and the roles themselves are not "good" or "bad." The inability to grow beyond the roles is what makes roles problematic in families affected by addiction. These roles carry over into other areas of life, making intimate relationships problematic, or careers/professional relationships difficult to navigate.

The **enabler** watches over, protects, and hides things to "help." The **hero** over-functions and is often perceived as being helpful within the family. The hero continuously strives to achieve approval and recognition. With much of the family attention directed to the hero, the **scapegoat** gains attention by acting out and getting in trouble. Negative attention is seen as better than receiving no attention at all. The **lost child** is shy, introverted, and withdrawn. To cope, the lost child turns inward and develops a fantasy life. The lost child is particularly vulnerable to the development of an addiction by using alcohol or drugs as a comfort. The **mascot** is funny, cute, and entertaining. When there is pain in the family, the mascot diverts attention through making light of the situation.

Test-Taking Strategies Applied

This is a recall question that relies on social workers understanding the effects of addiction on the family system and other relationships. Addiction has a profound impact on the relationships within families. The question also contains a qualifying word—MOST. As the child may be taking on another role, the behaviors described are frequently depicted by the scapegoat.

Knowledge Area

Unit I—Human Development, Diversity, and Behavior in the Environment (Content Area); Human Behavior in the Social Environment (Competency); Addiction Theories and Concepts (KSA)

55. C

Rationale

The inclusion of **spirituality** within social work is supported by ethical mandates. Cultural competence includes the need to understand spiritual values, beliefs, and traditions of clients. Spiritual beliefs help clients understand the world around them and give greater meaning to life. Social workers must view priests, rabbis, and other spiritual leaders as essential parts of clients' natural support networks. They must be utilized as resources to assist clients, with social workers providing education and emotional/physical support when needed.

Test-Taking Strategies Applied

The question requires the social worker to "most appropriately address the client's request." It contains a qualifying word—most—even though this word is not capitalized. Two of the response choices—informing her that the behavior is typical and asking why she thinks spirits are helpful—do not directly address the client's request.

It is inappropriate for the social worker to advise the client that the spiritual leader will not be helpful. It is most appropriate for the social worker to help the client prepare for the meeting by organizing her thoughts and questions.

Knowledge Area

Unit I—Human Development, Diversity, and Behavior in the Environment (Content Area); Diversity, Social/Economic Justice, and Oppression (Competency); The Principles of Culturally Competent Social Work Practice (KSA)

56. C

Rationale

The concept of **parallel process** has its origin in the psychoanalytic concepts of transference and countertransference. The transference occurs when social workers recreate the presenting problem and emotions of the therapeutic relationship within supervisory relationships. Countertransference occurs when supervisors respond to social workers in the same manner that social workers respond to clients. Thus, the supervisory interaction replays, or is parallel with, the therapeutic interaction.

Universalization is a communication technique used by social workers to normalize or generalize client beliefs, feelings, or behaviors to reduce clients' feelings of isolation. **Differential diagnosis** is the process of weighing the possibility that a client has one condition over another condition, as both conditions may have the same symptomology. **Suppression** is a client's ability to stop thinking negative thoughts or gain control over undesirable urges or beliefs.

Test-Taking Strategies Applied

This is a recall question that relies on social workers understanding transference and countertransference and how it can be manifested in supervisory relationships. Parallel process is an unconscious identification with a client and can be used as an important part of the supervisory process. Examining it will assist social workers and their supervisors to identify issues that exist in a therapeutic relationship so that they can be discussed and resolved.

Knowledge Area

Unit IV—Professional Relationships, Values, and Ethics (Content Area); Professional Development and Use of Self (Competency); The Impact of Transference and Countertransference Within Supervisory Relationships (KSA)

57. B

Rationale

Delirium tremens is a term for symptoms sometimes seen 3 to 10 days after abrupt **alcohol withdrawal** following heavy use. It is characterized by clinical confusion, sensory overload, and hallucinations, requiring hospitalization and treatment with medication. The presence of these symptoms is considered an emergency and needs immediate attention.

Test-Taking Strategies Applied

This is a recall question that relies on social workers understanding the use of, abuse of, and dependency on substances, including alcohol. It is essential for social workers to understand the indicators of substance abuse, as well as the signs of withdrawal. Making sure that the withdrawal symptoms—some of which can be life-threatening—are addressed takes precedence over developing strategies for long-term relapse prevention.

Knowledge Area

Unit I—Human Development, Diversity, and Behavior in the Environment (Content Area); Human Behavior in the Social Environment (Competency); Addiction Theories and Concepts (KSA)

58. C

Rationale

Concurrent planning is done by child welfare agencies and is the process by which an **interdisciplinary or intradisciplinary team** plans with children, youth, and families to reunite them while simultaneously considering and preparing to implement other permanency plans, such as adoption. It is a process that involves concurrent rather than sequential permanency planning efforts. It involves a mix of meaningful family engagement, targeted case practice, and legal strategies aimed at achieving timely permanency, while at the same time establishing and actively working a concurrent permanency plan in case the primary goal cannot be accomplished in a timely manner.

Test-Taking Strategies Applied

This is a recall question that relies on social workers knowing how teams in child welfare develop appropriate intervention plans that maximize the likelihood of positive outcomes for children. Collaborative approaches are critical to ensuring coordinated care and that all necessary issues are addressed. Teams are especially effective in complex situations such as those seen in child welfare.

Knowledge Area

Unit III—Interventions With Clients/Client Systems (Content Area); Intervention Processes and Techniques (Competency); Permanency Planning (KSA)

59. D

Rationale

Social work practice uses **multiple modalities, including individual, family, and group therapy**, to assist clients in resolving problems. Some clients may receive only one type of treatment, whereas others may engage in multiple modalities simultaneously or in succession. Each modality has advantages and may be preferred depending on the needs of and problems experienced by clients. A critical factor in deciding which is best is identifying the root cause of the problem. If a client is distressed about his or her own life circumstances and would like assistance in changing them, individual therapy would be appropriate.

Groups can act as a support network, and members of a group often come up with specific ideas for improving difficult situations or life challenges. Because members have different personalities and backgrounds, they look at situations in different ways. By seeing how other people tackle problems and make positive changes, group members can discover a whole range of strategies for facing their own concerns. Members realize that they are not the only ones struggling with the problem.

Individual and group therapy can be used in conjunction with one another. In this case scenario, the client is experiencing some problematic behaviors that may best be discussed in individual counseling, but she could also benefit from meeting others in similar situations to reduce her isolation.

Test-Taking Strategies Applied

The question contains a qualifying word—BEST. Although any of the incorrect response choices may be helpful, her needs are most effectively addressed by participation in both individual and group counseling. The use of both can assist the client to discuss her unique struggles with handling caregiving in a manner that is confidential and more personal (via individual counseling) while obtaining the support of others to reduce her isolation (via group counseling).

Knowledge Area

Unit III—Interventions With Clients/Client Systems (Content Area); Intervention Processes and Techniques (Competency); The Criteria Used in the Selection of Intervention/Treatment Modalities (e.g., Client/Client System Abilities, Culture, Life Stage) (KSA)

60. B

Rationale

Although there are many reporting formats available to social workers when **documenting in client records**, a SOAP format is particularly useful if an identified problem requires an intervention. The acronym SOAP represents these elements:

S—*Subjective information* describes how a client feels about or perceives a situation. It is derived from client self-reports. By definition, subjective information does not lend itself to independent or external validation.

O—*Objective information* is that which has been obtained by way of direct observation, clinical examinations, systematic data collection, and so on. As compared to subjective information, this category of information can be independently verified.

A—*Assessment* refers to a social worker's conceptualization or conclusions derived from reviewing the subjective and objective information.

P—*Plan* spells out how a specific problem will be addressed or resolved.

Test-Taking Strategies Applied

This is a recall question that relies on social workers knowing specific tools for assisting with writing and maintaining client records. There is no one way to organize information in client files. Often, requirements are dictated by funding sources and agency standards. However, it is essential that a set schema be established within the setting so social workers and their colleagues can access information quickly and accurately. It is also essential that files are secure, up-to-date, and complete.

Knowledge Area

Unit III—Interventions With Clients/Client Systems (Content Area); Documentation (Competency); The Principles and Features of Objective and Subjective Data (KSA)

61. B

Rationale

Crisis is an essential component in the understanding of human growth and development. Crisis situations are viewed as unusual—mostly negative—events that tend to disrupt life. A client's existing coping strategies may not be possible or may not be working effectively.

A crisis is an upset to a steady state. When a stressful event becomes a crisis, an individual or family is vulnerable and feels mounting anxiety, tension, and disequilibrium. A *precipitating event of a crisis does not have to be a major event*. It may be the "last straw" in a series of events that exceed a client's ability to cope.

An individual or family, at this point, may be emotionally overtaxed, hopeless, and incapable of effective functioning or making good choices and decisions. *The person or family is at a "critical turning point" of coping effectively or not effectively.*

Test-Taking Strategies Applied

The question requires social workers to understand the nature of crises. The correct answer can be identified through the process of elimination. A crisis does not need to be a major life event. Crisis intervention is also immediate and often brief—not long term. It aims to assist a client to regain equilibrium and return to his or her previous functional state. A crisis does not always involve a personal loss, but it can. Other life circumstances can also trigger a crisis.

Knowledge Area

Unit III—Interventions With Clients/Client Systems (Content Area); Indicators and Effects of Crisis and Change (Competency); Crisis Intervention Theories (KSA)

62. D

Rationale

Different drugs have different physical effects, so there are many **behavioral and physical signs** of drug dependency. Some physical signs include bloodshot eyes or pupils larger or smaller than usual, sudden weight loss or weight gain, deterioration of physical appearance, tremors, slurred speech, or impaired coordination.

Mood swings are associated with drug use, but are not a physical sign, as asked by the question. Mood swings are behavioral or psychological effects of dependency.

Test-Taking Strategies Applied

The question contains a qualifying word—NOT—that requires social workers to select the response choice that is not a physical sign of drug dependency. When NOT is used as a qualifying word, it is often helpful to remove it from the question and eliminate the three response choices that are physical signs. This approach will leave the one response choice that is NOT a physical sign.

Careful reading of the question is needed, as mood swings are a behavioral or psychological, rather than a physical, effect, making it the correct answer.

Knowledge Area

Unit II—Assessment (Content Area); Assessment Methods and Techniques (Competency); The Indicators of Addiction and Substance Abuse (KSA)

63. B

Rationale

When examining changes within organizations or the broader environment in which they operate, **SWOT analyses** can help determine the likely risks and rewards. SWOT, which stands for Strengths, Weaknesses, Opportunities, and Threats, is an analytical framework that can help organizations face their greatest challenges and chart courses for new directions. These analyses are also done by businesses to determine product development and viability. SWOT's primary objective is to help organizations develop a full awareness of all the factors, positive and negative, that may affect strategic planning and decision making. It is a precursor to taking any action.

Test-Taking Strategies Applied

The question contains a qualifying word—FIRST. There may be more than one appropriate response choice, but the order in which they are to occur is critical, with the most immediate or urgent happening first. It is essential that the social worker do an assessment to understand the impact of the other new agencies and determine why the level of service has dropped. Results may lead to actions in one of the other response choices, but first an evaluation needs to be done.

Knowledge Area

Unit II—Assessment (Content Area); Assessment Methods and Techniques (Competency); Methods to Assess the Client's/Client System's Strengths, Resources, and Challenges (e.g., Individual, Family, Group, Organization, Community) (KSA)

64. B

Rationale

Permanency planning is a social work practice philosophy that promotes a permanent living situation for every child entering the foster care system with an adult with whom the child has a continuous, reciprocal relationship and within a minimum amount of time.

Test-Taking Strategies Applied

This is a recall question that relies on social workers knowing about minors and self-determination, including those in the child welfare system.

Knowledge Area

Unit III—Interventions With Clients/Client Systems (Content Area); Intervention Processes and Techniques (Competency); Permanency Planning (KSA)

65. C

Rationale

Listening is the sensory capacity of social workers to receive and register the messages expressed verbally and nonverbally by clients. Most people are poor listeners and competent listening rarely comes naturally. For clients who are "experiencing a high degree of emotion" (e.g., upset), it is essential that they feel accepted and understood by social workers. Silence demonstrates to clients that social workers value and are interested in what they are saying and experiencing. It gives them "a safe space" to express themselves. By not interrupting or redirecting them, clients perceive that they can continue to express their feelings.

Test-Taking Strategies Applied

The question contains a qualifying word—MOST. Although all of the response choices may be acceptable actions by a social worker, the most effective in showing acceptance is remaining silent. Asking, explaining, and validating can be useful in gathering additional information about the situation or letting the client know that she is not alone as the social worker is there to help. However, acceptance is best achieved through what the social worker does (or does not do!) rather than what the social worker says.

Knowledge Area

Unit III—Interventions With Clients/Client Systems (Content Area); Intervention Processes and Techniques (Competency); Verbal and Nonverbal Communication Techniques (KSA)

66. B

Rationale

Communication is far more than an exchange of words. Facial expressions, hand gestures, posture, eye contact, and even silence are constantly sending messages about attitudes, emotions, status, and relationships. Nonverbal cues are critical.

Communication is culturally based. In order to be effective with those from diverse cultural, racial, and/or ethnic groups, a social worker must recognize direct and indirect communication styles and demonstrate sensitivity to nonverbal cues.

The client may be uncomfortable asking for help. The inability to meet basic needs may be accompanied by shame. There is no indication in the case scenario that the client is resistant, angry, or fearful.

Test-Taking Strategies Applied

The question contains a qualifying word—MOST. Although all of the response choices may be true, hesitancy and a lack of eye contact are likely associated with shame—not anger or fear. While they may be indicators of resistance, there is no indication that there is a resistance to receiving services as the client has come seeking assistance from the social worker.

Knowledge Area

Unit I—Human Development, Diversity, and Behavior in the Environment (Content Area); Diversity, Social/Economic Justice, and Oppression (Competency); The Effect of Culture, Race, and Ethnicity on Behaviors, Attitudes, and Identity (KSA)

67. C

Rationale

Social workers who work with couples and families must be aware of special **confidentiality** considerations. A key consideration for social workers who receive requests to release records in these instances is how records were created and maintained. If records related to services conjointly provided to both parties were maintained in one file, then consent to release the joint record is needed from both members of the couple. Records of services provided individually to each member if created and maintained separately can be released based on consent from the member who is the subject of the record.

If one party to the couple does not consent to the disclosure of records requested, the social worker is obligated to protect the confidentiality of both parties by refusing to release the information.

Test-Taking Strategies Applied

This is a recall question as social workers must be well versed in appropriate confidentiality practices, including those which have special considerations such as serving couples and families. Consent of one member of a couple is not adequate when a single record was created and maintained of services provided to both parties. Even when a social worker has made a referral to another service provider, proper consent procedures are needed to ensure confidentiality of information.

Knowledge Area

Unit IV—Professional Relationships, Values, and Ethics (Content Area); Confidentiality (Competency); Legal and/or Ethical Issues Regarding Confidentiality, Including Electronic Information Security (KSA)

68. A

Rationale

A **cost–benefit analysis** determines the financial costs of operating a program as compared with the fiscal benefits of its outcomes. A cost–benefit ratio is generated to determine whether, and the extent to which, the costs exceed the benefits. Program decisions can be made to eliminate or modify the program (by reducing program expenditures) based upon the findings. Often, the services delivered by social workers produce social value, but identifying the fiscal benefits can be challenging. If a client has increased self-esteem, it is difficult to know the accompanying monetary outcomes that result—such as increased wage earnings that result from career advancement due to an enhanced likelihood of self-promotion.

Isolating program costs and determining the evaluation period are necessary, but not the greatest challenge. Client permission may not be needed because this type of analysis is usually done on an aggregate basis without looking at specific client-level data.

Test-Taking Strategies Applied

This is a recall question that relies on social workers' knowledge of program evaluation techniques, namely cost–benefit analysis. As per the question, the greatest challenge has to be identified, which means that answers can be problematic, but the biggest obstacle has to be chosen as the correct response.

Knowledge Area

Unit III—Interventions With Clients/Client Systems (Content Area); Intervention Processes and Techniques (Competency); Methods, Techniques, and Instruments Used to Evaluate Social Work Practice (KSA)

69. B

Rationale

Preserving the **confidentiality of client documents** is a serious issue. Filing **"under seal"** is a procedure allowing sensitive or confidential information to be filed with a court without becoming a matter of public record. The court generally must give permission for the material to remain under seal. Filing confidential documents "under seal," separated from the public records, allows information to have greater protections of confidentiality.

Pro se is when a person represents himself or herself in legal proceedings without a lawyer.

Habeas corpus is a recourse in law whereby a person can report an unlawful detention or imprisonment before a court, usually through a prison official.

An **order of protection,** also known as a restraining order, is used by a court in cases of domestic violence, stalking, and harassment. It requires the adverse party to refrain from certain actions and requires that certain tasks be undertaken. Failure to comply is a violation of the order and the victim can request that the police and/or the court be involved to enforce the order more closely or take other action, depending on the severity of the violation.

Test-Taking Strategies Applied

This is a recall question that relies on social workers understanding the legal issues regarding confidentiality and, specifically, mechanisms for keeping sensitive information private.

Knowledge Area

Unit IV—Professional Relationships, Values, and Ethics (Content Area); Confidentiality (Competency); Legal and/or Ethical Issues Regarding Confidentiality, Including Electronic Information Security (KSA)

70. A

Rationale

Reaction formation is the fixation in consciousness of an idea, affect, or desire that is opposite to a feared, unconscious impulse. A mother who bears a child from an unwanted pregnancy may react to her feelings of guilt for not wanting to become pregnant by becoming extremely solicitous and overprotective to convince both the child and herself that she is a good mother.

Dissociation is the mental splitting of feelings or behaviors that are not wanted or acceptable.

Conversion is when a repressed urge is expressed as a disturbance in a body function. **Displacement** is directing an impulse, wish, or feeling toward a less threatening target.

Test-Taking Strategies Applied

The question contains a qualifying word—MOST. Although the client may be using other defense mechanisms, her behavior is probably related to her underlying feelings about the pregnancy. The question intentionally includes that the pregnancy was unwanted. The client's *actions are the opposite of what would be expected* based upon these feelings—which is a hallmark of reaction formation.

Knowledge Area

Unit I—Human Development, Diversity, and Behavior in the Environment (Content Area); Human Behavior in the Social Environment (Competency); Psychological Defense Mechanisms and Their Effects on Behavior and Relationships (KSA)

71. A

Rationale

Groupthink occurs when a homogenous highly cohesive group is so concerned with maintaining unanimity that they fail to evaluate all their alternatives and options. Groups engaged in groupthink tend to make faulty decisions when compared to the decisions that could have been reached using a fair, open, and rational decision-making process. Groups that engage in groupthink tend to fail to adequately determine their alternatives and select or use only information that supports their position and conclusions. Group leaders can prevent groupthink by encouraging members to raise objections and concerns.

Psychodrama is a treatment approach in which roles are enacted in a group context. **Interdependence** is a function of group cohesion whereby members are dependent upon one another for achievement of common goals. **Homogeneity** is the similarity of group members, which is another factor related to group cohesion.

Test-Taking Strategies Applied

The question contains a qualifying word—LIKELY. The question describes a problem or concern—that is, the ability of group members to consider alternatives and options. Thus, the answer must be linked to a pitfall in group functioning. Although all the response choices are related to group work, only the correct one is a problem, which serves as a clue. Unanimity, or wanting all members to be in agreement (at the expense of considering alternate views), concerns the thinking or thought processes of members and is another indicator that can be used to identify the correct answer.

Knowledge Area

Unit I—Human Development, Diversity, and Behavior in the Environment (Content Area); Human Behavior in the Social Environment (Competency); Theories of Group Development and Functioning (KSA)

72. **A**

Rationale

Protected classes are groups of people with common characteristics who are legally protected from employment discrimination on the basis of those characteristics. Federal protected classes are created by antidiscrimination law. Federal protected classes include race, color, religion, national origin, sex (or gender), age (over 40), and disability. Other groups, such as those with criminal histories, may be protected under state laws, but this question focuses on federal protections.

Test-Taking Strategies Applied

The question contains a qualifying word—EXCEPT. Its use indicates that all, but one, are protected classes. Knowledge of discrimination laws is helpful for discerning the correct answer. It is widely known that discrimination based on race or disability cannot occur. National origin discrimination involves treating people unfavorably because they are from a particular country or part of the world, because of ethnicity or accent, or because they appear to be of a certain ethnic background (even if they are not). Linking national origin to race or ethnicity may make its elimination as an incorrect answer easier.

Discriminating based on prior arrests, convictions, or incarcerations also is not appropriate, but appears to be the best choice based upon the answers provided.

Knowledge Area

Unit I—Human Development, Diversity, and Behavior in the Environment (Content Area); Diversity, Social/Economic Justice, and Oppression (Competency); Systemic (Institutionalized) Discrimination (e.g., Racism, Sexism, Ageism) (KSA)

73. A

Rationale

The *Tarasoff* decision refers to *Tarasoff v. Regents of the University of California*—decided by the California Supreme Court in 1976. It relates to the duty of mental health professionals when they determine (or should have determined) that a client is dangerous. In 1974, the California Supreme Court stated in *Tarasoff* that there is a **"duty to warn"** prospective victims. A subsequent ruling in 1976 reads that when it is determined "that his patient presents a serious danger of violence to another, he incurs an obligation to use reasonable care to protect the intended victim." This court further ruled that: "The discharge of this duty may require the therapist to . . . warn the intended victim or others likely to apprise the victim of the danger, to notify the police, or to take whatever steps are reasonably necessary under the circumstances."

Duty to warn means that a social worker must verbally tell the intended victim that there is a foreseeable danger of violence. Duty to protect implies a social worker determines that his or her client presents a serious danger of violence to another and is obligated to use reasonable care to protect the intended victim against danger. This may entail a warning, police notification, or other necessary steps.

Test-Taking Strategies Applied

This is a recall question that relies on social workers understanding the legal issues regarding confidentiality and, specifically, when reporting of a client's emotional status or behavior to others is required. On the examination, there are usually very few proper names related to laws, theories, and so on. However, the *Tarasoff* decision is an exception because it legally imposed the duty to warn and the duty to protect obligation on social workers.

Knowledge Area

Unit II—Assessment (Content Area); Assessment Methods and Techniques (Competency); Risk Assessment Methods (KSA)

74. **D**

Rationale

The **strengths perspective** is based on the assumption that clients have the capacity to grow, change, and adapt. Clients are the experts about their own lives. A strength is any ability that helps a client deal with a stressful life situation and use the challenging situation as a stimulus for growth. The recognition that there is a problem and the willingness to seek help is considered a strength. Strengths can include, but are not limited to, cognitive abilities, coping mechanisms, personal attributes, interpersonal skills, ethnic traditions, kinship bonds, or external resources.

Strengths vary from one situation to another and are contextual. They are dynamic—not static. A strength in one situation may not be a strength in another. In addition, strengths can emerge or dissipate over the life course.

Test-Taking Strategies Applied

The question contains a qualifying word—NOT—that requires social workers to select the response choice that is not true about the strengths perspective. When NOT is used as a qualifying word, it is often helpful to remove it from the question and eliminate the three response choices that are essential principles or true about strengths-based theory. This approach will leave the one response choice that is NOT an assumption.

Knowledge Area

Unit III—Interventions With Clients/Client Systems (Content Area); Intervention Processes and Techniques (Competency); Strengths-Based and Empowerment Strategies and Interventions (KSA)

75. **A**

Rationale

Professional development refers to skills and knowledge attained for effective service delivery. Professional development encompasses all types of learning opportunities, ranging from formal course work and conferences to informal learning opportunities situated in practice. There are a variety of approaches to professional development, including *consultation, coaching, communities of practice, mentoring, reflective supervision, and technical assistance.*

Test-Taking Strategies Applied

Response choices should always be viewed through the lens of what is best for a client. Self-determination of clients is only limited in situations that would cause harm to clients or others. The correct response choice is always the one that puts clients first. The professional development of social workers benefits clients by the provision of effective service delivery. Two of the response choices talk about requirements for licensure or career advancement, which may be real. However, they are not directly related to client care. The last answer speaks about serving more clients. Serving all those in need is critical, but it is more essential to ensure that social workers are meeting the needs of the clients they currently have before acquiring new ones.

There is also a qualifying word—BEST—that is capitalized in the question. The use of this qualifying word indicates that more than one of the provided response choices may be correct, but selecting the one that is most important is key. Making sure that clients receive effective services is paramount to professional practice.

Knowledge Area

Unit IV—Professional Relationships, Values, and Ethics (Content Area); Professional Development and Use of Self (Competency); Professional Development Activities to Improve Practice and Maintain Current Professional Knowledge (e.g., In-Service Training, Licensing Requirements, Reviews of Literature, Workshops) (KSA)

76. D

Rationale

The social worker must address the client's fears about her son's future. Two of the response choices are directed at intervening with the son— one indirectly by setting goals for him, and one directly by meeting with him. The son is not the client, so these interventions are not appropriate.

One of the answers relies on **self-disclosure** by the social worker as a way of instilling hope. Most therapeutic situations require no self-disclosure by a social worker. In fact, a client having information about a social worker's family, personal interests, and/or relationship status can be an indication of a potential boundary violation. Prior to disclosing any information about themselves, social workers should engage in consultation or supervision about why such disclosure is being considered and why it is professionally justified in this instance. Only when it will clearly assist clients and *there are no other methods for achieving the same outcome* should it be contemplated. Self-disclosure in this case scenario is not needed because there are other methods for addressing the client's fears.

Finding out from the client about her aspirations for her son is a step toward exploring and addressing her concerns. Her belief that her son will "never amount to anything" based on his arrest requires the social worker to better understand the basis of her comments. It is unclear if she is worried about the existence of a criminal record negatively affecting the attainment of his educational or employment goals or other concerns that may have been the causes of his delinquent behavior, such as poor impulse control or judgment.

Test-Taking Strategies Applied

The question contains quotation marks that provide a clue to the correct answer. Quotation marks in the question often are the key to distinguishing between the correct answer and the incorrect one. Wording in quotes is there for a reason and usually points to the KSA being tested or other critical information. In this case scenario, the social worker's action must address the fear being expressed.

Knowledge Area

Unit IV—Professional Relationships, Values, and Ethics (Content Area); Professional Development and Use of Self (Competency); Self-Disclosure Principles and Applications (KSA)

77. B

Rationale

Social workers may discover the presence of **human trafficking**. Often victims do not seek help voluntarily, but may need medical or other critical services. They are often fearful to accept help and will not self-identify, so knowing the indicators is important. Some of these "red flags" are mentioned in the question.

Social workers must alert law enforcement immediately as it is unsafe to attempt to rescue victims as the trafficker may react and retaliate. For urgent situations, social workers should notify local law enforcement immediately, but should also alert the National Human Trafficking Resource Center, which has a 24-hour, toll-free multilingual hotline to ensure response by law enforcement officials knowledgeable about human trafficking.

Social workers should not attempt to meet with other victims due to safety issues or conduct investigations themselves. Offering services to address immediate needs may be helpful, but victims may be placed with different agencies who specialize in working with victims to address long-term effects of this exploitation; this often accompanies other forms of abuse.

Test-Taking Strategies Applied

This is a recall question as social workers must be aware of human trafficking and other forms of exploitation. Understanding the social work role when indicators exist for this abuse is essential to ensure its proper handling. Social workers should not conduct investigations as they are best handled by law enforcement authorities. Often victims of human trafficking are viewed as criminals themselves, hence the creation of a special hotline.

Social workers must always be aware of actions that jeopardize their safety and should minimize risk.

Knowledge Area

Unit II—Assessment (Content Area); Concepts of Abuse and Neglect (Competency); The Indicators, Dynamics, and Impact of Exploitation Across the Lifespan (e.g., Financial, Immigration Status, Sexual Trafficking) (KSA)

78. C

Rationale

Pansexual is a term that has become more common in recent years as a way for some to better identify their **sexual identities**. Pansexual is derived from the Greek prefix "pan," meaning "all." The term is reflective of those who are attracted to others regardless of their gender identity or biological sex, including those who are male, female, transgender, intersex, and so on. Pansexual recognizes gender fluidity and attraction to those who may not be gender binary.

Test-Taking Strategies Applied

This is a recall question that relies on social workers understanding diverse gender and sexual identities. The question contains a qualifying word—likely—that is not capitalized. The client's use of pansexual probably indicates an attraction to those with varying gender and/ or sexual identities. However, social workers should not make any assumptions; rather, they must let clients explain their identities, which may vary even when the same labels are used.

Knowledge Area

Unit I—Human Development, Diversity, and Behavior in the Environment (Content Area); Diversity, Social/Economic Justice, and Oppression (Competency); Sexual Orientation Concepts (KSA)

79. D

Rationale

All **communication** has two aspects: receptive language and expressive language. Receptive language is the ability to listen and understand language. Expressive language is the ability to communicate with others using language. These two facets of language are very different, but equally important.

When children begin to talk, their receptive language skills are usually much more advanced than their expressive language skills. At about 4 years old, most children have an expressive vocabulary of about 2,300 words, but a receptive language vocabulary of about 8,000 words. When a baby responds to the sound of a pleasant voice, the baby is displaying the beginnings of receptive language. When a baby coos in response to a familiar voice, the baby is beginning to use expressive language. These are signs that the baby is beginning to understand that communication is important and useful.

Test-Taking Strategies Applied

The question contains a qualifying word—TRUE. It is even capitalized to assist with identifying the distinguishing factor of the correct response from the rest. Each statement must be read carefully and evaluated as to its accuracy. The correct answer is identified through a process of elimination, with each false assertion being excluded.

Knowledge of language development in childhood is required to obtain the correct answer.

Knowledge Area

Unit II—Assessment (Content Area); Assessment Methods and Techniques (Competency); Communication Theories and Styles (KSA)

80. B

Rationale

Social workers focus on assisting clients to **identify problems** and areas of strength, as well as increasing problem-solving strategies. It is essential that, throughout the problem-solving process, *social workers view clients as experts in their lives*. Clients should be asked what they would like to see changed in their lives and clients' definitions of problems should be accepted. Clients should be asked about the paths that they would like to take to make desired changes. Clients' perceptions should be respected and clients' inner resources (strengths) should be maximized as part of treatment.

In this case scenario, there is no information about whether the client recognizes any of the issues listed as important or why she is seeking services at this time. This information is critical to driving assessment, planning, and intervention. Finding out, from the client, what she would like to change is a fundamental part of engagement, which starts in the first meeting.

Test-Taking Strategies Applied

The question contains a qualifying word—FIRST. There may be more than one appropriate response choice, but the order in which they are to occur is critical. In this case scenario, the social worker is meeting with the client for the first time. The inclusion of the qualifying word, FIRST, coupled with it being the initial session makes the correct response choice the action that initiates their relationship. Often, social workers lead off initial discussions in the first meeting with, "Why are you here?" There is information about problems that the client is having, but her reasons for seeking treatment may relate to other issues or only one of those mentioned.

Knowledge Area

Unit II—Assessment (Content Area); Assessment Methods and Techniques (Competency); Methods of Involving Clients/Client Systems in Problem Identification (e.g., Gathering Collateral Information) (KSA)

81. A

Rationale

Trauma is how the mind responds to stressful life events. Emotional and psychological trauma involves *painful feelings* and *frightening thoughts* invoked by witnessing or experiencing a traumatic event. Although most process and deal with these feelings after a short time, some are unable to do so.

The strong feelings brought on by trauma can cause extreme behavior. Sleep disturbance, withdrawal, detachment, flashbacks, nightmares, and feelings of intense helplessness and fear are some of the symptoms endured by victims of trauma.

Test-Taking Strategies Applied

The question requires social workers to know the effects of trauma. The signs are seen in everyday life and can include physical problems such as racing heartbeat, fatigue, muscle tension, and so on. However, they are best assessed by speaking with clients. Understanding clients' thoughts and feelings is essential to determining the impacts of these stressful life events on well-being.

Knowledge Area

Unit II—Assessment (Content Area); Assessment Methods and Techniques (Competency); Methods Used to Assess Trauma (KSA)

82. D

Rationale

Lithium is a prescription medication used for the treatment of a mental health issue: Bipolar Disorder. Lithium blood levels are often measured during the process of determining a client's optimum dosage. A client's age, health, and other medications can affect what level of lithium is best for him or her. Long-term lithium use can affect the kidneys and thyroid. Blood work is typically ordered when a client begins lithium therapy and periodically afterward to help keep the dosage at the proper level. Blood work is also ordered when a client taking lithium experiences unusual side effects or begins taking other medications to determine how they may be affecting the client's blood levels.

Test-Taking Strategies Applied

This is a recall question that relies on social workers understanding medical monitoring that accompanies the taking of prescription medications for mental and behavioral disorders. The question also contains a qualifying word—MOST. A client may need to have some of the tests listed as incorrect response choices, but the use of lithium requires bloodwork to ensure the achievement of therapeutic drug levels and to monitor toxicity.

Knowledge Area

Unit II—Assessment (Content Area); Assessment Methods and Techniques (Competency); Common Psychotropic and Non-Psychotropic Prescriptions and Over-the-Counter Medications and Their Side Effects (KSA)

83. B

Rationale

The primary goal of **social work case management** is to optimize functioning and well-being by providing and coordinating high-quality services, in the most effective and efficient manner possible, to clients with multiple complex needs. Although case management can include various tasks, there are five core activities: (a) assessing, (b) planning, (c) linking, (d) monitoring, and (e) advocating. Counseling is *not* typically done as part of social work case management and is not an essential activity.

Test-Taking Strategies Applied

The question contains a qualifying word—NOT—that requires social workers to select the activity that is not a core function of case management. When NOT is used as a qualifying word, it is often helpful to remove it from the question and eliminate the three response choices that are essential case management activities. This approach will leave the one response choice which is NOT required.

Knowledge Area

Unit III—Interventions With Clients/Client Systems (Content Area); Intervention Processes and Techniques (Competency); The Components of Case Management (KSA)

84. C

Rationale

Congruent communication occurs when the same message is sent verbally and nonverbally. In this case scenario, the verbal report of the client does not match her actions. Thus, the social worker should employ **interviewing techniques** to determine the reason.

The aim of a social work interview is to gather important information and keep clients focused on the achievement of goals. **Confrontation** is not implicitly punitive, but instead calls attention to issues, including inconsistencies in client behavior. Other interviewing techniques include reflecting, validating, clarifying, paraphrasing, interpreting, and so on.

Test-Taking Strategies Applied

In the case scenario, the presenting issue is the incongruence between the client's verbal report and her actions. Several of the incorrect response choices do not directly address the issue—focusing on one aspect of the case scenario (e.g., her level of enjoyment) rather than the case scenario in its entirety. One incorrect answer assumes that her absences and disinterest are caused by resistance. The only way to determine the reason for the inconsistency is to speak to the client directly. The interview should call attention to or confront the issue in an effort to understand the client's thoughts and feelings better.

Knowledge Area

Unit II—Assessment (Content Area); Assessment Methods and Techniques (Competency); The Concept of Congruence in Communication (KSA)

85. C

Rationale

Somatic symptoms are medically unexplained physical symptoms that can be associated with mental and emotional illness. A mental disorder based on somatic symptoms can last for years and result in substantial impairment. In the *DSM-5*, Somatization Disorder, Hypochondriasis, Pain Disorder, and Undifferentiated Somatoform Disorder have been eliminated, with many, but not all, clients previously diagnosed with one of these disorders now being diagnosed with Somatic Symptom Disorder (SSD). Somatic symptoms often result in frequent medical visits in spite of negative investigations. SSD can be associated with a great deal of stigma as there is a risk that clients may be dismissed by their physicians as having problems that are "all in their head." However, it should not be seen as a malingering condition that can be controlled.

Test-Taking Strategies Applied

This is a recall question that relies on social workers understanding the symptoms of mental and emotional illness across the lifespan. Although somatic complaints may be associated with trauma and stress, they also can be associated with SSD. SSD occurs when a client feels extreme anxiety about physical symptoms such as pain or fatigue. The client has intense thoughts, feelings, and behaviors related to the symptoms that interfere with daily life. The client is not faking the symptoms. The pain and other problems are real. They may be caused by a medical problem, but no physical cause can be found. It is the extreme reaction and behaviors about the symptoms that are the main problem.

Knowledge Area

Unit II—Assessment (Content Area); Assessment Methods and Techniques (Competency); The Indicators of Somatization (KSA)

86. D

Rationale

Imaginary friends often emerge during **Piaget's preoperational stage** (2–7 years old) and may last into elementary school. Although children do interact with them, most know that their friends are not real and only pretend they are real. Thus, having an imaginary friend in childhood does not indicate the presence of a disorder. It is a typical part of development and social workers should normalize behavior with parents who are distressed about this activity during this developmental stage.

The mother's concern comes from a lack of knowledge about cognitive development and, thus, the way "to best assist" is to provide **psychoeducation**. Only the correct response choice focuses on education. The son does not appear to also be a client in the case scenario, so meeting with him is not appropriate. Since having an imaginary friend is not an indicator of a mental health concern or loneliness, there is no need to evaluate further or find other playmates for him.

Test-Taking Strategies Applied

This question requires selecting the answer that is the way "to best assist." It is important to examine the answers as they relate to helping the client directly. Some response choices involve intervening with the son, who does not appear to be a client. Other answers focus on assessment tasks, but an intervention is most closely linked to assisting.

Knowledge Area

Unit III—Interventions With Clients/Client Systems (Content Area); Intervention Processes and Techniques (Competency); Psychoeducation Methods (e.g., Acknowledging, Supporting, Normalizing) (KSA)

87. B

Rationale

Ego strength is the ability to be exposed to different types of stress and tolerate them. One client's strength may be another's weakness. Clients who have resiliency also have ego strength. Resiliency is a client's ability to overcome adversity and challenges. Thus, the relationship is positive, meaning high amounts of ego strength are associated with high amounts of resiliency and vice versa. On the other hand, a negative or inverse relationship implies that high values of one concept are associated with low values on the other. A curvilinear relationship changes over time, being positive for some period and negative at others.

Test-Taking Strategies Applied

The question contains a qualifying word—BEST. It requires knowledge about coping skills, as well as relationships in research. A client with well-developed ego strength is resilient, optimistic, and has a strong sense of self, which allows him or her to be capable in handling challenges. A healthy ego strength is connected to a healthy self-concept. A client who is resilient can look at a situation and see beyond it. This information eliminates the presence of a negative or inverse relationship. There are times when the relationship between ego strength and resiliency may be stronger or can fluctuate, but the most apt way to describe this association is positive.

Knowledge Area

Unit II—Assessment (Content Area); Assessment Methods and Techniques (Competency); The Indicators of Client's/Client System's Strengths and Challenges (KSA)

88. B

Rationale

In this case scenario, missed appointments, which can be a sign of resistance or a lack of motivation to engage in the intervention process, did not occur in the past. This behavior emerged during **termination**, at the end of the problem-solving process. Thus, it is probably resulting from the client placing other activities and responsibilities as priorities. The client should not be blamed for such behavior and it does not mean that old problems continue or new problems have emerged. The client is likely not angry.

The meetings may be losing their value or importance to the client because the problem has been resolved. The social worker should not drag on services longer than needed.

Test-Taking Strategies Applied

The question contains a qualifying word—MOST. Although some of the response choices may be accurate, missed appointments during termination, especially when this client behavior has not been seen in the past, are associated with clients not seeing the utility in formal termination sessions. In the case scenario, substantial progress had been made and there is no indication that a new problem had emerged. Since termination had begun, both the client and social worker acknowledged the appropriateness of ending the services.

Knowledge Area

Unit III—Interventions With Clients/Client Systems (Content Area); Intervention Processes and Techniques (Competency); The Indicators of Client/Client System Readiness for Termination (KSA)

89. D

Rationale

Globalization is the growing interdependence of societies across the world. Globalization has a profound effect on social work practice as it impacts (differentially) on the work opportunities and living conditions of populations. Therefore, it changes service delivery and influences thinking about welfare policies. It also creates new social problems for social workers to address, such as human trafficking and environmental issues.

Test-Taking Strategies Applied

The question contains a qualifying word—PRIMARY—that indicates that globalization may be a concern for social workers for reasons listed in the incorrect response choices. However, the correct answer can be distinguished from the others as it relates to the impact of globalization on clients—not social workers. The primary concern of social workers is always clients and disparities in treatment that may cause inequalities.

Knowledge Area

Unit I—Human Development, Diversity, and Behavior in the Environment (Content Area); Diversity, Social/Economic Justice, and Oppression (Competency); The Impact of the Environment (e.g., Social, Physical, Cultural, Political, Economic) on Individuals, Families, Groups, Organizations, and Communities (KSA)

90. A

Rationale

According to the *NASW Code of Ethics*, social workers in **fee-for-service settings** may terminate services to clients who are not paying an overdue balance if the financial contractual arrangements have been made clear to a client, if a client does not pose an imminent danger to self or others, and if the clinical and other consequences of the current nonpayment have been addressed and discussed with a client. The social worker also provided alternate resources to meet the client's need, making the actions ethical.

Test-Taking Strategies Applied

In practice, social workers often have to make subjective judgments about how the *NASW Code of Ethics* should be applied. On the examination, social workers should adhere to the "facts" provided rather than about what they may want to do. In this case scenario, the question focused on whether the actions were ethical—not whether they were optimal or desired. Material in the *NASW Code of Ethics* about termination in fee-for-service settings states that such termination may take place as long as the financial arrangement, including consequences for nonpayment, are understood by the client and the client is not a danger to self or others. Both of these conditions have been met in the case scenario.

Knowledge Area

Unit IV—Professional Relationships, Values, and Ethics (Content Area); Professional Values and Ethical Issues (Competency); Legal and/or Ethical Issues Related to Termination (KSA)

91. **C**

Rationale

Based on systems theory, the client's physical limitations will likely impact on his psychological, emotional, and social well-being. The **interplay of biological, psychological, social, and other factors** is a critical concern. Social workers are keenly aware of this interconnection and recognize that changes in any one domain will impact on others.

The assessment phase is driven by a biopsychosocial–cultural–spiritual evaluation. The first two incorrect responses may be useful, but do not recognize a systems approach and are not critical to fully understanding the implications of his recent diagnosis. The last incorrect answer is not an activity that occurs during the assessment phase as it is an intervention that happens later in the problem-solving process (engaging, assessing, planning, intervening, evaluating, and terminating).

Test-Taking Strategies Applied

The question contains a qualifying word—MOST. Although it may be useful to find out the etiology of his physical disability and where he is in the development process, the greatest concern must be the impact of his limitations on other life domains.

The correct answer recognizes a cornerstone of the social work profession, namely the interplay between biological, psychological, social, cultural, and spiritual factors.

Knowledge Area

Unit II—Assessment (Content Area); Biopsychosocial History and Collateral Data (Competency); Biopsychosocial Responses to Illness and Disability (KSA)

92. **C**

Rationale

A **culturagram** is an essential tool for social workers to use when assessing clients' cultural backgrounds. It gives the social worker an opportunity to *understand client culture on an individual basis rather than generalizing to the cultural group*. It was developed to be used as an assessment tool to help social workers and others understand families from different cultural backgrounds, including immigrants. It helps to understand that culture is a very broad concept and is different for everyone, even within the same cultural groups. The culturagram works from a strengths-based perspective. It is meant for clients and social workers to see clients' cultures as unique as a way to empower them.

The following are considered: reason for relocation; legal status; time in community; language spoken at home and in the community; health beliefs; impact of trauma and crisis events; contact with cultural and religious institutions; holidays, food, and clothing; oppression, discrimination, bias, and racism; values about education and work; and values about family-structure, power, myths, and rules.

Test-Taking Strategies Applied

This question seeks to understand the impact of the cultural environment on client systems. It is important for social workers to be knowledgeable about various cultures. Attending continuing education, using outside resources, and speaking to others may be helpful, but the only way to understand the impact to a particular client is by direct assessment, using a tool such as the culturagram. A client's experiences may be very different from a social worker's, and there is a danger in viewing them through a worker's own personal lens.

Knowledge Area

Unit II—Assessment (Content Area); Biopsychosocial History and Collateral Data (Competency); The Components of a Biopsychosocial Assessment (KSA)

93. A

Rationale

Opioids are prescription painkillers such as OxyContin, Percocet, and Vicodin, as well as the street drug heroin. Many people first use opioids when they are prescribed to them by dentists or doctors for pain associated with removal of teeth or injuries. Common prescription opioids include codeine (an ingredient in some prescription cough syrups and pain relievers), Fentanyl, hydrocodone, Vicodin, oxycodone, Percocet, and Darvocet.

Medication-assisted treatment is the use of medication, along with therapy and other supports, to help address issues related to opioid dependence, including withdrawal, cravings, and relapse prevention.

Test-Taking Strategies Applied

The question contains a qualifying word—MOST. It is possible that the client was addicted to other substances listed, but the only opioid is heroin.

Social workers must be familiar with the signs of use and abuse of substances, as well as understand treatment options.

Knowledge Area

Unit I—Human Development, Diversity, and Behavior in the Environment (Content Area); Human Behavior in the Social Environment (Competency); Addiction Theories and Concepts (KSA)

94. D

Rationale

Social workers often rely on the expertise of others to assist in determining the causes and treatment of client problems. In these instances, social workers may have to make **referrals** to other professionals with specialized knowledge and skills. The *NASW Code of Ethics* has some ethical standards with regard to whom social workers can refer and how such referrals should be made (*NASW Code of Ethics, 2008—2.06 Referral for Service*). It mandates that social workers refer clients to other professionals when the other professionals' specialized knowledge or expertise is needed to serve clients fully or when social workers believe that they are not being effective or making reasonable progress with clients and that additional service is required. In addition, it requires social workers who refer clients to other professionals to take appropriate steps to facilitate an orderly transfer of responsibility, including disclosing, with clients' consent, all pertinent information to the new service providers.

In this case scenario, the social worker is fee splitting or receiving payment for a referral when no professional service is provided by the referring social worker. This practice is prohibited by the *NASW Code of Ethics*. Even though the social worker is not receiving the money directly, she is gaining directly through the receipt of training and/or indirectly by allowing her agency to receive assistance. This is unethical.

Test-Taking Strategies Applied

Whenever a question requires judgment about ethical behavior, answers should be assessed based on the standards in the *NASW Code of Ethics*. In real life, there are often factors that cause ethical dilemmas or result in interpretation of the standards based on circumstances present. The correct answer on the examination is usually the one that most closely mirrors the actual relevant standard in the *NASW Code of Ethics*.

Knowledge Area

Unit III—Interventions With Clients/Client Systems (Content Area); Use of Collaborative Relationships (Competency); Consultation Approaches (e.g., Referrals to Specialists) (KSA)

95. D

Rationale

The **stages of loss and grief** are universal and are experienced by clients from different cultural backgrounds. Mourning occurs in response to clients' own terminal illnesses or disabilities, the loss of close relationships, death or disability of family members or friends, and so on. There are five stages of typical grief that were first proposed by Elisabeth Kübler-Ross in 1969. They are denial and isolation, anger, bargaining, depression, and acceptance. Clients spend different lengths of time working through each step and express each stage with different levels of intensity. The five stages do not necessarily occur in any specific order. Clients often move between stages, finally gaining a greater degree of acceptance.

Throughout each stage, a common thread of hope emerges. Hope is not a separate stage, but possible during any stage.

Test-Taking Strategies Applied

This is a recall question that relies on social workers understanding the dynamics and effects of loss, separation, and grief. Loss, separation, and grief can occur at any time, and each client will be unique in how he or she copes with these issues. However, there are five typical stages that characterize the process.

Knowledge Area

Unit III—Interventions With Clients/Client Systems (Content Area); Indicators and Effects of Crisis and Change (Competency); The Dynamics and Effects of Loss, Separation, and Grief (KSA)

96. A

Rationale

Active listening is a social work interview technique that helps clients feel heard and understood. Active listening involves the combination of talking and listening skills to show clients that social workers are active and collaborative participants in service delivery and helps convey empathy for clients' problems or situations.

During active listening, **mirroring or paraphrasing** techniques are used to reflect back what has been said. Each response needs to be tailored to what clients are saying to demonstrate that social workers are truly listening and engaged in what is being revealed.

Test-Taking Strategies Applied

The question contains a qualifying word—MOST. Active listening does not focus on questioning clients or assessing their problems. It is also not about interpreting what is being said. Active listening can be used during any step in the problem-solving process as a method to build or strengthen the relationships between social workers and their clients.

Knowledge Area

Unit III—Interventions With Clients/Client Systems (Content Area); Intervention Processes and Techniques (Competency); The Principles of Active Listening and Observation (KSA)

97. C

Rationale

There are many myths about suicide, including that there are no warning signs before a client commits suicide. In addition, many falsely believe that a client who attempts suicide and survives is unlikely to make another attempt. There are numerous **risk factors for suicide**, including a history of previous attempts, being isolated and lacking social supports, substance abuse, family history of suicide, experiencing a recent loss, and so on. One less known risk factor is a *sudden improvement in client well-being* or a lifting of his or her spirits. This behavior often is an indication that a client has made a firm decision to commit suicide and feels better because of this choice. In addition, in the 3 months following an attempt, a client is at most risk of another attempt to commit suicide.

Test-Taking Strategies Applied

The question contains a qualifying word—MOST. It is possible, but unlikely, that the client's change in affect is due to one of the incorrect response choices. The change occurred "suddenly," which makes it improbable that it resulted from decreased isolation or enhanced coping skills, both of which would produce changes more gradually over time.

Although antidepressants start to work immediately within the brain, clients may not notice the effects until some later time. It is generally accepted that all antidepressants have a delayed onset of action (the length of time needed for a medication to become effective)—with no major effects seen until after at least 3 weeks of treatment. However, antidepressants at effective doses produce partial improvements in some clients within 1 to 2 weeks of treatment. In summary, the effects of antidepressants are gradual and would not produce the sudden improvement in mood mentioned in the case scenario.

Knowledge Area

Unit III—Interventions With Clients/Client Systems (Content Area); Indicators and Effects of Crisis and Change (Competency); The Indicators and Risk Factors of the Client's/Client System's Danger to Self and Others (KSA)

98. A

Rationale

Ego strength is the ability to effectively deal with the demands of the id, the superego, and reality. It is a basis for resilience and helps maintain emotional stability by coping with internal and external stress. Strong ego strength describes clients who first accept whatever raised their frustration tolerance, then look at it and explore it with a view to dealing with, coping, and mastering it. With ego strength, clients do not personalize things that happen in the world or what others say. As ego strength grows, clients develop stronger senses of self and ability to handle whatever comes (e.g., **coping skills**).

Traits usually considered to be indicators of positive ego strength include tolerance of pain associated with loss, disappointment, shame, or guilt; forgiveness of others, with feelings of compassion rather than anger; persistence and perseverance in the pursuit of goals; and/or openness, flexibility, and creativity in learning to adapt. Those with positive ego strength are less likely to have psychiatric crises.

Test-Taking Strategies Applied

This is a recall question that relies on social workers understanding Sigmund Freud's three parts of the personality—the id, the ego, and the superego. The **id** is entirely unconscious and includes instinctive and primitive behaviors. The id is driven by the pleasure principle, which strives for immediate gratification of all desires, wants, and needs. The **ego** is responsible for dealing with reality. The ego operates based on the reality principle, which strives to satisfy the id's desires in realistic and socially appropriate ways. The **superego** provides the sense of right and wrong.

Knowledge Area

Unit II—Assessment (Content Area); Assessment Methods and Techniques (Competency); The Indicators of Client's/Client System's Strengths and Challenges (KSA)

99. C

Rationale

Change is difficult and often frightening, so it is reasonable to expect many clients to evidence occasional signs of **resistance** with treatment plans that attempt to induce some change. Psychodynamic models view resistance as part of the therapeutic process—the result of clients' ongoing conflict with a consciously professed desire to change and their unconscious fears about losing their safe ground and sense of identity.

Rather than viewing client resistance merely as an annoying impediment, social workers do well to look at client resistance as providing important information that can shape the assessment and intervention, as well as increase social workers' empathy and effectiveness in selecting an individualized approach.

Resistance does not result from poor performance by social workers, and is not an impediment to effective service delivery. It can happen at any time in the problem-solving process.

Test-Taking Strategies Applied

The question contains a qualifying word—MOST. Although some information in the incorrect response choices may be accurate, in order for resistance to be "effectively" used, it must assist social workers in some way in the problem-solving process. The incorrect answers view resistance as bad—something that is an impediment. Its value must be recognized in order for it to be used constructively.

Knowledge Area

Unit II—Assessment (Content Area); Assessment Methods and Techniques (Competency); Methods to Assess Motivation, Resistance, and Readiness to Change (KSA)

100. C

Rationale

Androgynous is a state in which gendered behaviors, presentations, and/or roles include aspects of both masculinity and femininity. People of any gender identity or sexual orientation can be androgynous.

Individuals who are **transsexual** feel that they are not the gender which they were assigned by birth and are treated with medical intervention, including gender reassignment surgeries and hormone therapy. Transgender is a larger umbrella term that includes those who are transsexual but also refers to those whose identity, expression, behavior, or general sense of self does not conform to what is usually associated with their biological gender at birth. Transgender, then, unlike transsexual, is a multifaceted term, encompassing those who consider themselves gender nonconforming, multigendered, androgynous, third gender, and two-spirit people.

Intersex refers to those who are born with genital ambiguity (e.g., their chromosomes do not match conventional men or women, nor do their genitals). They can identify as male, female, or neither, and may choose to surgically change their genitals or not.

Cross dressing is the act of wearing items of clothing and other accoutrements commonly associated with the opposite sex within a particular society. Cross dressing has been used for purposes of disguise, comfort, and self-actualization. The case scenario describes other characteristics, such as hair and makeup, which are not associated with apparel.

Test-Taking Strategies Applied

This is a recall question that relies on social workers' understanding of terms associated with gender identity and expression, sexual orientation, and related topics. This case scenario relates to gender expression. There is no information about his gender identity. Gender expression and gender identity are distinct concepts that may or may not be congruent.

Knowledge Area

Unit I—Human Development, Diversity, and Behavior in the Environment (Content Area); Diversity, Social/Economic Justice, and Oppression (Competency); Gender and Gender Identity Concepts (KSA)

101. D

Rationale

Peer supervision differs from more traditional forms of supervision in that it does not require the presence of a more qualified, identified expert in the process. Peer supervision usually refers to reciprocal arrangements in which peers work together for mutual benefit, developmental feedback is emphasized, and self-directed learning and evaluation is encouraged. Some of the benefits of peer supervision include increased access to or frequency of supervision, *reciprocal learning* through the sharing of experiences, increased skills and responsibility for *self-assessment*, and decreased dependency on expert supervisors.

Peer supervision also has a number of potential pitfalls. Groups can lack structure and degenerate into gossip sessions or discussion groups. Peer supervision may be more threatening than one-on-one supervision processes, with social workers not feeling safe enough to expose their needs in a group setting. Lastly, the clinical skills within the group also may not be sufficient to handle the service challenges presented.

Test-Taking Strategies Applied

The question contains a qualifying word—NOT—that requires social workers to select the response choice that is not a pitfall of peer supervision. When NOT is used as a qualifying word, it is often helpful to remove it from the question and eliminate the three response choices that are pitfalls or disadvantages of peer supervision. This approach will leave the one response choice that is NOT a drawback.

Knowledge Area

Unit IV—Professional Relationships, Values, and Ethics (Content Area); Professional Development and Use of Self (Competency); Models of Supervision and Consultation (e.g., Individual, Peer, Group) (KSA)

102. C

Rationale

The social worker's comment is a "positive" **stereotype,** which is just as damaging as a negative one. A stereotype is a widely held but fixed and oversimplified image or idea of a person or thing.

A common stereotype is that those who are Asian are smart. However, some who are Asian, like those in all other races or ethnicities, are not smart. Using "positive" stereotypes sets a standard for people living under those stereotypes to reach, even when it is not possible. Thus, people can be hurt by "positive" stereotypes just as they can be hurt by negative ones.

Test-Taking Strategies Applied

The social worker states that the client is smart, "as expected," and then justifies his expectation to the client's race. When words are in quotation marks in questions, they should be considered carefully—they are included for a reason. In this case scenario, they highlight a belief that qualifies as a stereotype.

It is the responsibility of the supervisor to assess the practices of the social worker. Even though the social worker may not see the harm imposed by his comment, it is unacceptable and must be addressed by the supervisor. Educating the client about the impact of his comments will hopefully prevent him from perpetuating them with others.

Knowledge Area

Unit I—Human Development, Diversity, and Behavior in the Environment (Content Area); Diversity, Social/Economic Justice, and Oppression (Competency); The Effects of Discrimination and Stereotypes on Behaviors, Attitudes, and Identity (KSA)

103. B

Rationale

The terms **life expectancy** and **lifespan** describe two distinctly different things, although they are often used interchangeably.

Life expectancy refers to the number of years a person is expected to live, based on a statistical average. This statistical average is calculated based on a population overall, including those who die during childbirth, shortly after childbirth, during adolescence or adulthood, and those who live well into old age.

A number of factors influence life expectancy, including gender, race, exposure to pollution, education status, income level, and health care access. Modifiable lifestyle factors such as exercise, alcohol status, smoking status, and diet also influence life expectancy. Therefore, life expectancy is highly variable from one individual to another.

Lifespan, on the other hand, refers to the maximum number of years that a person can potentially expect to live based on the greatest number of years anyone has lived. Taking humans as the example, the oldest documented age reached by any living individual is about 122 years, meaning humans are said to have a lifespan of about 122 years.

Test-Taking Strategies Applied

This question requires social workers to have information about the relationship between life expectancy and human life span. It is critical to be able to tease out what is being stated about life expectancy and the human lifespan separately in each of the response choices and weigh its accuracy. Understanding the distinction between the two terms is important for selecting the correct answer.

Knowledge Area

Unit I—Human Development, Diversity, and Behavior in the Environment (Content Area); Human Growth and Development (Competency); Theories of Human Development Throughout the Lifespan (e.g., Physical, Social, Emotional, Cognitive, Behavioral) (KSA)

104. C

Rationale

Age-related diseases are illnesses and conditions that occur more frequently in people as they get older, meaning age is a significant risk factor. Examples of age-related diseases are:

- Cardiovascular disease (heart disease is the number one killer in the United States, with the most common form being coronary artery disease)

- Cerebrovascular disease (strokes can cause death or disability and happen when blood stops flowing in one area of the brain because of a disruption in one of the blood vessels)
- Hypertension (chronically elevated blood pressure can cause serious problems for the heart, blood vessels, kidneys, and other systems in the body)

Cancer, type 2 diabetes, Parkinson's disease, and dementia are also age-related diseases.

Rates of gastroesophageal reflux disease (GERD) do not increase with age, but esophageal symptoms of sufferers become more severe as they get older.

Test-Taking Strategies Applied

The question contains a qualifying word—NOT—that requires social workers to select the response choice that is not a health condition that increases in frequency as people age. When NOT is used as a qualifying word, it is often helpful to remove it from the question and eliminate the three response choices that are age-related health conditions. This approach will leave the one response choice that is NOT linked to age.

Knowledge of the health issues facing older adults is critical to being able to select the correct answer.

Knowledge Area

Unit I—Human Development, Diversity, and Behavior in the Environment (Content Area); Human Growth and Development (Competency); The Indicators of Normal and Abnormal Physical, Cognitive, Emotional, and Sexual Development Throughout the Lifespan (KSA)

105. C

Rationale

Systems theory describes human behavior in terms of complex systems. It states that an entire system changes when one part of a system is altered. Social workers are trained to understand the relationships between biological, psychological, social, spiritual, and cultural aspects of well-being. For example, when a client becomes physically disabled, this impairment is likely to impact on social connections, relationships, self-image, and so on.

Psychodynamic theory was developed by Freud, and it explains personality in terms of conscious and unconscious forces. It describes the personality as consisting of the id (responsible for following basic instincts), the superego (attempts to follow rules and behave morally), and the ego (mediates between the id and the superego).

Social learning theory is based on Bandura's idea that learning occurs through observation and imitation. New behavior will continue if it is reinforced. The learning process is also more efficient if the new behavior is modeled.

Psychosocial development theory is an eight-stage theory of identity and psychosocial development articulated by Erikson. Erikson believed everyone must pass through stages of psychosocial development over the life cycle, ranging from infancy to older adulthood.

Test-Taking Strategies Applied

The question contains a qualifying word—BEST. Although some of the other theories may relate to the interplay of biological, psychological, social, and spiritual factors, the relationship between these domains is most aptly described by systems theory. It explains the interconnectedness between all aspects of client well-being. Understanding the linkage between them is essential for proper assessment and intervention.

Knowledge Area

Unit I—Human Development, Diversity, and Behavior in the Environment (Content Area); Human Growth and Development (Competency); The Interplay of Biological, Psychological, Social, and Spiritual Factors (KSA)

106. C

Rationale

The most common **antidepressants** prescribed to clients are those belonging to a class called selective serotonin reuptake inhibitors (SSRIs). Prozac is an SSRI and works by preventing the reuptake (movement back into the nerve endings) of a neurotransmitter called serotonin. Low levels of serotonin have been associated with depression, so it is believed that SSRIs relieve depression by making more of this important substance available for use. SSRIs are generally preferred by doctors and patients over the older classes of antidepressants—monoamineoxidase inhibitors (MAOIs) and tricyclics—because they have fewer side effects and are relatively safe in overdose.

Haldol and Clozaril are used for the treatment of psychosis, such as that associated with Schizophrenia. Lithium is prescribed for those with Bipolar Disorder as it is a mood stabilizer.

Test-Taking Strategies Applied

The question contains a qualifying word—MOST. Although the client in the case scenario may be prescribed some of the other medications for comorbid disorders, Prozac is the only antidepressant listed, making it the correct answer.

Knowledge Area

Unit II—Assessment (Content Area); Assessment Methods and Techniques (Competency); Common Psychotropic and Non-Psychotropic Prescriptions and Over-the-Counter Medications and Their Side Effects (KSA)

107. A

Rationale

Social workers focus on assisting clients in **problem identification** while viewing clients as experts in their lives. Even when clients are referred, clients should be asked what they would like to see changed in their lives, and clients' definitions of problems should be accepted. The reasons that clients enter a social service system often differ from the issues that are most concerning to them.

In this case scenario, the social worker should check with his or her colleague to find out the reason for the referral. Knowing this information may provide some insight into the immediate need. However, more importantly, the client must be asked about pressing concerns, as they may be different from the reasons for the referral. There are multiple issues listed in the case scenario, but it is unknown if any of them are the reasons for the referral or the client's true concerns.

Test-Taking Strategies Applied

The question contains a qualifying word—FIRST. There are many problems listed, but the reason for the referral and what issues are of concern to the client are unknown. The social worker can obtain the views of the colleague about the presenting problem, but will not know if this view matches the concerns of the client until after the first meeting. The actions listed in the incorrect response choices may all be done, but only after the social worker establishes the presenting problem. Problem identification drives assessment and intervention and must always come first in the process.

Knowledge Area

Unit II—Assessment (Content Area); Assessment Methods and Techniques (Competency); Methods of Involving Clients/Client Systems in Problem Identification (e.g., Gathering Collateral Information) (KSA)

108. B

Rationale

Clients are often reluctant to reveal **sensitive information** about themselves and others in their families. However, this information may be vital to understanding client problems and designing interventions that will be effective. While there is no set road map of how to elicit this information, a social worker should start off with some open-ended, nonthreatening questions to gather needed background and get a client used to talking about his or her situation before having to disclose more sensitive issues.

This initial questioning will also give a client time to "test the waters" with a social worker and gauge his or her reaction as more sensitive information is provided. Trust is often needed in a therapeutic relationship before a client can be completely honest about his or her situation. A client is much more likely to disclose sensitive information if a social worker reacts to such disclosures with acceptance and a neutral stance, being neither judgmental nor confrontational and not interrupting when information is being gathered.

Test-Taking Strategies Applied

The question is testing knowledge about social work interviewing techniques. In the case scenario, the "social worker believes that knowing more about the abuse will provide insight into her problems, but is reluctant to bring it up." If the material is valuable to assisting the client to understand her current problems, the social worker must move beyond feeling uncomfortable with eliciting sensitive information. Perhaps the client *does* want to discuss her past sexual abuse but is worried that the social worker will judge her or feel awkward. It is important for the client to understand that the abuse is not her fault, but simply stating that will not elicit the information needed to better understand the client's history. Getting more detail is useful, but the social worker must broach this topic with sensitivity—using open-ended and nonthreatening questions—or the client may shut down.

Knowledge Area

Unit III—Interventions With Clients/Client Systems (Content Area); Intervention Processes and Techniques (Competency); Methods to Obtain Sensitive Information (e.g., Substance Abuse, Sexual Abuse) (KSA)

109. C

Rationale

There are different **types of developmental/maturational and situational crises**. Developmental crisis results from a typical life change (e.g., puberty, leaving home, marriage, birth of children, retirement, etc.). These are changes that are part of life and can only be successfully transitioned through as a client learns to cope with his or her situation.

Situational crisis results from unexpected trauma such as that resulting from death of a family member or friend, illness, or displacement. Because of the unexpected shock, a client typically experiences these events as more stressful. At times, developmental and situational crises can occur simultaneously.

Test-Taking Strategies Applied

The question contains a qualifying word—NOT—that requires social workers to select the response choice that is a situational as opposed to a maturational crisis. Situational crises are not expected as part of typical development. Puberty, marriage, and retirement are anticipated in the life course, whereas the death of a child is not.

Knowledge Area

Unit III—Interventions With Clients/Client Systems (Content Area); Indicators and Effects of Crisis and Change (Competency); Crisis Intervention Theories (KSA)

110. D

Rationale

At times, a social worker may need to use a **sign language interpreter** when working with a client. A social worker should always use a qualified, trained interpreter—not a client's family member or friend—in order to assure accuracy, confidentiality, and objectivity in the process. Extra time should be built into an interview with a client using an interpreter to allow time for translation. A client needs to know that information provided via interpretation will remain confidential because trained interpreters must also adhere to confidentiality standards.

Test-Taking Strategies Applied

In the case scenario, the client has experienced problems thought to be tied to miscommunication. It is essential that the social worker accurately understand the client's circumstances. If the client regularly uses American Sign Language (ASL) to communicate, the social work interview must be done using ASL. The ability of the client to hear amplified speech does not mean that she can articulate her needs verbally. She may need ASL for expressive communication. Using family members or friends is not appropriate, and the client should not have to go to another agency. Referring her elsewhere places additional burden on the client when her communication needs can be easily met with some accommodation. Rather than proceeding immediately, it is better to wait for another meeting at which ASL interpretation can be provided.

Knowledge Area

Unit I—Human Development, Diversity, and Behavior in the Environment (Content Area); Diversity, Social/Economic Justice, and Oppression (Competency); The Principles of Culturally Competent Social Work Practice (KSA)

111. A

Rationale

There are two main **types of evaluations**—formative and summative. A **formative evaluation** usually takes place during program implementation as it *examines the processes* as they occur in an attempt to determine which are promoting and/or inhibiting successful outcomes. Information gathered from a formative evaluation may help to identify changes in program provisions that can increase their efficiency and/ or effectiveness. This information is vital to the decision making of administrators and managers. A **summative evaluation** is focused on determining a program's effectiveness or *examining its outcomes*. A summative evaluation provides valuable data at a program's completion to determine whether it should be continued, modified, or eliminated.

Research designs are experimental, quasi-experimental, or nonexperimental. **Experimental research** is usually conducted in restricted settings, such as laboratories, to control extraneous variables, making generalization of findings difficult. The main advantage of experimental designs is that they provide the opportunity to identify cause-and-effect relationships. **Nonexperimental research** (e.g., case studies, surveys, and correlation studies) is usually conducted in natural settings. **Quasi-experimental research** mirrors experimental design, but lacks a key ingredient, random assignment.

Test-Taking Strategies Applied

The question contains a qualifying word—BEST. Although some of the response choices may be helpful in making decisions, formative evaluations are optimally suited for this purpose as they occur during program implementation and examine the processes as they occur in an attempt to assess whether they are promoting or inhibiting program goals.

Knowledge Area

Unit III—Interventions With Clients/Client Systems (Content Area); Intervention Processes and Techniques (Competency); Methods, Techniques, and Instruments Used to Evaluate Social Work Practice (KSA)

112. B

Rationale

Despite fears about **client records** being ordered for release without client consent, there is clear necessity to meet professional practice standards, third-party payer requirements, and ethical guidelines by preparing and maintaining accurate and timely records.

Social workers may inappropriately feel that they should not document for fear that information may be released by court order without client consent. Although discretion is required when determining what to include and how to phrase assessments and findings, there is strong support for accurate treatment records that demonstrate commitment to professional practice standards.

Test-Taking Strategies Applied

The correct answer can be identified through the process of elimination. None of the incorrect response choices are accurate. Social workers should not omit important information from records just because it may be harmful to clients if released. Records are to be safeguarded and social workers should take actions to protect their release without client consent. However, all relevant information, in detail needed to ensure service continuity and evaluation, must be recorded.

Professional opinions, which are supported with subjective and objective data, may be contained in client records if they are relevant to the problem-solving process and address the problem(s) at hand. Lastly, not all records are stored electronically, so they may not contain information about practices to safeguard electronic information.

Knowledge Area

Unit IV—Professional Relationships, Values, and Ethics (Content Area); Confidentiality (Competency); The Use of Client/Client System Records (KSA)

113. C

Rationale

Means-testing **eligibility criteria** target services to those who are low income. In the United States, means-tested welfare programs provide cash, food, housing, medical care, social services, training, and targeted education to those who are poor. Means-tested government programs differ from other government programs in two important ways. First, they provide aid exclusively to clients (or communities) with low incomes; second, clients do not need to earn eligibility for benefits through prior fiscal contributions. Means-tested welfare, therefore, does not include Social Security, Medicare, unemployment insurance, or workers' compensation.

Test-Taking Strategies Applied

This is a recall question that relies on social workers knowing criteria for determining and maintaining clients' eligibility for services. Social workers play an important role in assisting clients to access services.

Although the incorrect response choices may be important in maintaining services generally (*using any eligibility criteria*), meeting financial criteria is the basis of means testing. Only the correct answer includes mention of fiscal qualifications.

Knowledge Area

Unit III—Interventions With Clients/Client Systems (Content Area); Use of Collaborative Relationships (Competency); The Effects of Policies, Procedures, Regulations, and Legislation on Social Work Practice and Service Delivery (KSA)

114. D

Rationale

Termination is the last step in the problem-solving process. Social workers should terminate services to and professional relationships with clients when such services and relationships are no longer required or no longer serve client needs or interests. Social workers should take reasonable steps to avoid abandoning clients who are still in need of services. Social workers should withdraw services precipitously only under unusual circumstances, giving careful consideration to all factors in the situation and taking care to minimize possible adverse effects. Social workers should assist in making appropriate arrangements for continuation of services when necessary.

During termination, the progress made during treatment/services should be reviewed and acknowledged. Termination should help a client anticipate the future, focusing on what to do if the problem reoccurs. The loss experienced by a client and social worker triggered by not closely working together in the future should also be recognized.

Informing the client of confidentiality standards is done at the beginning and throughout earlier steps in the problem-solving process as needed. Reiterating them during termination is not necessary as a client should be familiar with the confidentiality standards. Developing a trusting therapeutic alliance from the onset of services relies on a client understanding confidentiality and its limits.

Test-Taking Strategies Applied

The question contains a qualifying word—EXCEPT. Three of the four response choices are necessary parts of termination in the problem-solving process. Social workers should read each answer and ask whether it must be done when services are ending. Confidentiality is important, but reiteration of the standards occurs earlier in the problem-solving process—not at termination.

Knowledge Area

Unit III—Interventions With Clients/Client Systems (Content Area); Intervention Processes and Techniques (Competency); Discharge, Aftercare, and Follow-Up Planning (KSA)

115. A

Rationale

Cognitive theory is based on the premise that unhelpful thinking results from dysfunctional beliefs and/or cognitive distortions. These thoughts, which are not supported by empirical evidence, result in automatically occurring bad habits. With practice and effort, clients can become more aware of what is happening in their minds and change how they are thinking for the better. **Cognitive restructuring**, also known as cognitive reframing, is a technique drawn from cognitive therapy that can help clients identify, challenge, and alter stress-inducing thought patterns and beliefs. These beliefs are altered by clients becoming aware of them as they occur and then criticizing and critiquing them. Usually, there is no logical or rational basis for their existence. Thus, when clients examine their judgments carefully, looking for evidence to support them, they find none. The end goal of cognitive restructuring is to enable clients to replace stress-inducing thought habits with more accurate and less rigid (and therefore less stress-inducing) thinking habits.

Test-Taking Strategies Applied

This is a recall question that relies on social workers being aware of cognitive interventions. Although the incorrect response choices are true statements, they do not justify the use of cognitive restructuring and are not rooted in cognitive theory. Only the correct answer gets to the rationale for why cognitive restructuring is a helpful hands-on technique to bring about change in clients.

Knowledge Area

Unit III—Interventions With Clients/Client Systems (Content Area); Intervention Processes and Techniques (Competency); Cognitive and Behavioral Interventions (KSA)

116. D

Rationale

Social work practice uses **multiple modalities**, including **individual, family, and group therapy**, to assist clients in resolving problems. Some clients may receive only one type of treatment, whereas others may engage in multiple modalities simultaneously or in succession. Each modality has advantages and may be preferred depending on the needs of and problems experienced by clients.

A critical factor in deciding which is best is identifying the root cause of the problem. In this case scenario, the client feels isolated, wanting opportunities to socialize and receive support. Groups can act as a support network and members of a group often come up with specific ideas for improving difficult situations or life challenges. Because members have different personalities and backgrounds, they look at situations from different perspectives. By joining a group of retirees, the client may obtain ideas about venues for meeting others, as well as use the group as a natural support network.

The client does not need vocational services because there is no expressed desire to return to work. Case management is appropriate for clients engaged with multiple service providers who need assistance navigating the system. Its use is not warranted in the case scenario provided. Lastly, individual counseling will not naturally connect her with others or reduce her isolation, which is the primary service need described.

Test-Taking Strategies Applied

The question contains a qualifying word—BEST. Although some of the services listed in the incorrect response choices may be helpful, participation in a group will be most beneficial to meeting the presenting problem—lack of socialization and support.

Knowledge Area

Unit III—Interventions With Clients/Client Systems (Content Area); Intervention Processes and Techniques (Competency); The Criteria Used in the Selection of Intervention/Treatment Modalities (e.g., Client/Client System Abilities, Culture, Life Stage) (KSA)

117. C

Rationale

Social workers are expected to communicate effectively, including in the preparation of **written reports for external organizations**. Poorly written reports or the inclusion of irrelevant or inappropriate information can have an adverse impact on a client. In the preparation of reports, including those for the courts, *social workers are expected to communicate accurately and professionally*. Critical to developing reports is the knowledge that they must be understandable and useful. Social workers should avoid irrelevant and inappropriate information, meaningless phrases or slang words, and illogical conclusions.

Social workers should not limit relevant information if it is court ordered. Social workers must be aware of confidentiality standards and inform clients of the need to release information prior to its release when feasible. A "document ordered by the court" is legally required to be submitted. However, when courts of law order social workers to disclose confidential or privileged information without client consent, and such disclosure could cause harm, social workers should request that courts withdraw the orders, limit the orders as narrowly as possible, or maintain the records under seal (i.e., unavailable for public inspection). However, social workers ultimately do not have control over what is done with the information once it is submitted to the courts. Thus, it can result in anticipated and unanticipated negative consequences.

Social workers should respond in a timely manner in all instances so the timeliness is not "the primary concern" in this situation.

Test-Taking Strategies Applied

The question contains a qualifying word—primary—even though this word is not capitalized. Social workers should submit information in a timely fashion, but cannot limit relevant information when legally required to release it. There is an ethical mandate for social workers to request that courts withdraw or narrow the scope of the orders that may cause harm to a client because there is ultimately no control over how such information is used once it is submitted. When developing or submitting court-ordered materials, social workers must make sure documents are well-written and concise and only contain information that is relevant to the main concern.

Knowledge Area

Unit III—Interventions With Clients/Client Systems (Content Area); Documentation (Competency); The Principles and Processes for Developing Formal Documents (e.g., Proposals, Letter, Brochures, Pamphlets, Reports, Evaluations) (KSA)

118. A

Rationale

The current definition under the Developmental Disabilities Assistance and Bill of Rights Act of 2000 defines **"developmental disability"** as a severe, chronic disability of an individual that:

- Is attributable to a mental or physical impairment or combination of mental and physical impairments
- Is manifested before the individual attains age 22
- Is likely to continue indefinitely
- Results in substantial functional limitations in three or more of the following areas of major life activity: self-care, receptive and expressive language, learning, mobility, self-direction, capacity for independent living, and economic self-sufficiency
- Reflects the individual's need for a combination and sequence of special, interdisciplinary, or generic services, individualized supports, or other forms of assistance that are of lifelong or extended duration and are individually planned and coordinated

In 1978, Congress raised the age of onset to 22, and switched from a list of specific conditions to a more generalized approach focused on a functional definition of a developmental disability as a "severe, chronic disability . . . attributable to a physical or mental impairment . . . likely to continue indefinitely" and resulting in substantial functional limitations in three or more areas of major life activity.

Test-Taking Strategies Applied

The question contains a qualifying word—NOT. Three of the four response choices are included in the federal definition. Although age 18 may seem likely to be included in a federal definition, due to its ties to emancipation in some states, educational entitlements for those requiring additional secondary schooling are provided through age 21.

Knowledge Area

Unit II—Assessment (Content Area); Biopsychosocial History and Collateral Data (Competency); Biopsychosocial Responses to Illness and Disability (KSA)

119. A

Rationale

The term *"trias politica"* or **separation of powers** was coined in the 18th century to assert that the most effective method for promoting liberty is to separate governmental powers and have them act independently. Separation of powers, therefore, refers to the division of government responsibilities among distinct branches and limitations on any one branch from exercising the core functions of another. The intent is to prevent the concentration of power and provide for checks and balances. The powers of the branches of American government are as follows:

- The legislative branch is responsible for enacting laws and appropriating the money necessary to operate the government.
- The executive branch is responsible for implementing and administering public policy enacted and funded by the legislative branch.
- The judicial branch is responsible for interpreting the constitution and laws and applying those interpretations to controversies brought before it.

Test-Taking Strategies Applied

The question contains a qualifying word—PRIMARY—that indicates that more than one answer choice applies to the separation of government into three branches, but the main reason for this structure must be selected from the rest.

Knowledge Area

Unit III—Interventions With Clients/Client Systems (Content Area); Use of Collaborative Relationships (Competency); The Relationship Between Formal and Informal Power Structures in the Decision-Making Process (KSA)

120. B

Rationale

According to the *NASW Code of Ethics*, social workers should not **terminate services** to pursue a social, financial, or sexual relationship with a client.

In this case scenario, the social worker agreed to terminate services in order to befriend the client. The client suggesting this termination or finding another appropriate service provider does not make this situation ethical. The amount of time that elapsed before the social worker saw the client also does not mitigate or eradicate this ethical breach.

Test-Taking Strategies Applied

This is a recall question that relies on social workers understanding the ethical and legal issues regarding termination. "Once a client, always a client" is a phrase used to remind social workers that the ethical standards of the profession and professional boundaries do not cease just because therapeutic relationships with clients have ended. Having social, financial, and sexual relationships with clients is prohibited, so it is, therefore, not appropriate to end services to pursue them.

Knowledge Area

Unit IV—Professional Relationships, Values, and Ethics (Content Area); Professional Values and Ethical Issues (Competency); Legal and/or Ethical Issues Related to Termination (KSA)

121. D

Rationale

Democratic is a social system based on the formal equality of rights and privileges. **Pluralistic** is the conviction that various religious, ethnic, racial, and political groups should be allowed to thrive in a single society. **Egalitarian** is the principle that all people are equal and deserve equal rights and opportunities. **Patriarchal** is the privilege and dominance of men over women. Patriarchal social systems are those in which men are in authority over women in all aspects of society. Some characteristics of a patriarchal system include:

- *Male dominance:* Men make all the decisions regarding both societal and family issues, hold all positions of power and authority, and are considered superior.
- *Male identification:* Values center around male qualities of control, strength, forcefulness, rationality, strong work ethic, and competitiveness.
- *Male centeredness:* The center of activity and attention is on male contributions (i.e., what they do to move the society forward).

Test-Taking Strategies Applied

This is a recall question that relies on social workers understanding types of social systems and their characteristics. Patriarchal systems are more common in certain cultures. Identifying their existence and understanding their impact on behaviors, attitudes, and identity is critical.

Knowledge Area

Unit I—Human Development, Diversity, and Behavior in the Environment (Content Area); Diversity, Social/Economic Justice, and Oppression (Competency); The Effect of Culture, Race, and Ethnicity on Behaviors, Attitudes, and Identity (KSA)

122. C

Rationale

A **genogram** is a family diagram that can be thought of as an elaboration of a family tree. Genograms provide a way of mapping family patterns and relationships. Genograms report information on family structures. Genograms are widely used by social workers as a tool to map family relations, giving both social workers and clients an overview of family issues, relationships, and patterns. Genograms can also be used to better understand their clients' medical and genetic histories.

Test-Taking Strategies Applied

This is a recall question that relies on social workers understanding family theories and dynamics. There is also a qualifying word—best— but it is not capitalized. Although a biopsychosocial–spiritual–cultural assessment may be helpful, its focus is not of the greatest assistance in understanding the family structure and relationships that should be the focal point of the tool selected.

Knowledge Area

Unit II—Assessment (Content Area); Biopsychosocial History and Collateral Data (Competency); The Types of Information Available From Other Sources (e.g., Agency, Employment, Medical, Psychological, Legal, or School Records) (KSA)

123. C

Rationale

A **power of attorney** is a written authorization that allows someone else the ability to make certain choices if a client is not available. "Power of attorney" does not mean that a client is involved in a legal matter or has given power to a lawyer; in fact, the person selected by a client does not need any legal experience.

Implementing a power of attorney does not mean that a client cannot make decisions. It allows someone else to act on his or her behalf if needed, such as due to hospitalization. The power of attorney is considered null or void upon a client's death. A client's will governs the handling of his or her estate, including decisions about assets.

Another type of power of attorney exists for those who become incapacitated and are not able to make decisions concerning their own financial affairs. This type of power of attorney is called a durable power of attorney. "Durable" simply means that the other person can act if or when a client becomes unable to do so, but that person is required by law to make the best decisions for the client—both financially and physically.

Test-Taking Strategies Applied

This is a recall question that relies on social workers knowing about competence and self-determination. Although several of the response choices may be true, only one can be assumed to be based upon the existence of a power of attorney. "True" is also a qualifying word—though it is not capitalized. It is essential to evaluate each answer separately to determine its veracity.

Knowledge Area

Unit IV—Professional Relationships, Values, and Ethics (Content Area); Professional Values and Ethical Issues (Competency); Client/Client System Competence and Self-Determination (e.g., Financial Decisions, Treatment Decisions, Emancipation, Age of Consent, Permanency Planning) (KSA)

124. A

Rationale

Troubled social workers who become involved in inappropriate client relationships often disclose personal information to clients because doing so helps cope with their own challenges. In the case scenario, the social worker did not disclose personal information to strengthen the therapeutic alliance or assist the client in any way. This **self-disclosure** was rooted in the social worker's own needs—his legal problems with settling his father's estate.

Self-disclosure issues in social work arise in various settings and circumstances. Many of these issues in clinical contexts involve some form of intimacy. Social workers should not disclose personal information to clients when such self-disclosure could produce tangible, material benefits or favors beyond monetary payment for services rendered. In this case scenario, the social worker's disclosure to a client who is a lawyer may have been rooted in seeking advice or guidance.

Providing this information is most directly linked to a boundary crossing, as confidentiality standards were not broken. It was the social worker providing information about himself—not a client. There were also no related consent or payment issues.

Test-Taking Strategies Applied

The question contains a qualifying word—PRIMARILY. Although there may be additional concerns related to the social worker–client relationship, the disclosure is most directly an indication of a dual relationship or boundary crossing.

Knowledge Area

Unit IV—Professional Relationships, Values, and Ethics (Content Area); Professional Development and Use of Self (Competency); Self-Disclosure Principles and Applications (KSA)

125. D

Rationale

Human development describes growth throughout the life course, from conception to death. The study of human development seeks to understand and explain how and why people change throughout their lives, including in the areas of physical, emotional, intellectual, social, perceptual, and personality development. This knowledge can be applied by social workers to help clients live up to their full potential.

With an awareness of how humans unfold developmentally, social workers can determine and anticipate where clients fit developmentally and where they are on the "maps" that usually guide the life course.

Test-Taking Strategies Applied

The question contains a qualifying word—MOST. Although knowledge of human development may be useful in identifying delays requiring intervention and/or assisting with understanding environmental effects, it is essential to determining what clients have already mastered and what can be expected in the future. Knowledge of human development forms the basis of all steps in the problem-solving process because social workers engage, assess, plan, and intervene using methods that are based on clients' cognitive, social, and emotional growth. Also, many problems that clients experience are caused by factors that negatively impact on typical development.

Knowledge Area

Unit I—Human Development, Diversity, and Behavior in the Environment (Content Area); Human Growth and Development

(Competency); Theories of Human Development Throughout the Lifespan (e.g., Physical, Social, Emotional, Cognitive, Behavioral) (KSA)

126. B

Rationale

Doctors cannot definitively diagnose **Alzheimer's disease** until after death, as the only truly definitive test for Alzheimer's is a brain biopsy, which is almost never done. Because brain biopsies are too invasive and risky, Alzheimer's usually gets diagnosed by systematically ruling out other common possibilities for the symptoms. Confusion and memory problems can stem from a host of things, including small strokes (so small the person may not show other signs of stroke), drug interactions or side effects, Parkinson's, thyroid problems, brain tumors, pernicious anemia, depression, low oxygen levels, high fluid pressures in the brain, and others. Alzheimer's is one of the most common causes of confusion in older adults, but not the only cause. Confusion is never a typical part of aging.

Test-Taking Strategies Applied

The question contains a qualifying word—BEST. Although the incorrect response choices may help in ruling out other possibilities, brain biopsies are the only method for definitively diagnosing Alzheimer's disease.

Knowledge Area

Unit II—Assessment (Content Area); Biopsychosocial History and Collateral Data (Competency); The Types of Information Available From Other Sources (e.g., Agency, Employment, Medical, Psychological, Legal, or School Records) (KSA)

127. A

Rationale

Role playing is a teaching strategy that offers several advantages. Role playing in social work practice may be seen between supervisor and supervisee or social worker and client. In all instances, role playing usually raises interest in a topic as supervisees or clients are not passive recipients in the learning process. In addition, role playing teaches empathy and understanding of different perspectives. In role playing, participation helps embed concepts. Role playing gives clarity to information that may be abstract or difficult to understand.

The use of role playing emphasizes personal concerns, problems, behavior, and active participation. *It improves interpersonal and communication skills and enhances communication.*

Test-Taking Strategies Applied

The correct answer is one that aims "to enhance the client's communication skills." Several of the incorrect answers are related to assessment or finding out more about the problem. However, the correct response choice must be an intervention. Arranging for a family session is an intervention, but it is not appropriate as the client would need to formulate his thoughts and communicate effectively. It is not that he has not had the opportunity to speak to his parents, but that he lacks the expressive communication skills to relay his feelings effectively. These skills can be learned and practiced in role play, which is a "safe" interaction between the client and social worker, before being used with his parents.

Knowledge Area

Unit III—Interventions With Clients/Client Systems (Content Area); Intervention Processes and Techniques (Competency); The Technique of Role Play (KSA)

128. A

Rationale

A **double-barreled question** is a single question that addresses more than one issue but only allows for one answer. Double-barreled questions result in confusion and inaccuracies in the answers received because there is no clarity as to which issue in the double-barreled question the respondent is expected to focus on.

The question in the case scenario is asking for one response to two separate issues, pay and job conditions. Its use may lead to inaccurate responses because employees may answer with "satisfied" while, in reality, they are "very satisfied" with the job conditions but "unsatisfied" with the pay.

Test-Taking Strategies Applied

The question contains a qualifying word—BEST. Some of the incorrect response choices may be true. For example, satisfaction may be assessed more precisely by including additional response choices, and employee input into survey development is optimal. However, they do not relate directly to a concern about this question. It is double barreled, causing confusion for employees who must respond. The lack of clarity jeopardizes the integrity of the information generated.

Knowledge Area

Unit III—Interventions With Clients/Client Systems (Content Area); Intervention Processes and Techniques (Competency); Methods, Techniques, and Instruments Used to Evaluate Social Work Practice (KSA)

129. D

Rationale

In communication, there are two types of content, manifest and latent. **Manifest content** is the concrete words or terms contained in a communication, whereas **latent content** is that which is not visible—the underlying **meaning of communication** (words or terms). Relying just on the manifest content to understand client experiences or problems may result in not really understanding their meaning to individuals.

    Reflective interviewing restates and explores client affective (feeling) messages. Social workers validate clients by conveying accurately an understanding of their feelings. This process leads to the establishment of rapport and the beginning of a therapeutic relationship.

    Nonverbal cues are methods of communication that do not involve words, including body movements, body orientation, eye contact, facial expression, dress, and so on.

Test-Taking Strategies Applied

This is a recall question that relies on social workers knowing how to identify the underlying meaning of communication. In the case scenario, the social worker is not directly interviewing the client or basing the assessment on nonverbal cues. The case notes contain manifest and latent content. Since the social worker is focusing "on underlying themes," the approach is based on latent, rather than manifest, communication.

Knowledge Area

Unit II—Assessment (Content Area); Assessment Methods and Techniques (Competency); Communication Theories and Styles (KSA)

130. A

Rationale

According to the *NASW Code of Ethics*, social workers should inform clients, to the extent possible, about the **disclosure of confidential information** and the potential consequences—when feasible, before the disclosure is made. This applies whether social workers disclose confidential information on the basis of a legal requirement or client consent. Following agency policy is always important from a practical perspective, but this question asks about guidance provided in the professional code of ethics. The *NASW Code of Ethics* is clear about the need to inform the client before the disclosure when feasible to do so.

Test-Taking Strategies Applied

This is a recall question that relies on social workers understanding the legal issues regarding confidentiality and, specifically, what to do when disclosure of confidential information must be released, such as suspected child abuse or the issuance of a court order.

Knowledge Area

Unit IV—Professional Relationships, Values, and Ethics (Content Area); Professional Values and Ethical Issues (Competency); Legal and/or Ethical Issues Regarding Mandatory Reporting (e.g., Abuse, Threat of Harm, Impaired Professionals, etc.) (KSA)

131. B

Rationale

Adult perpetration of abuse remained strongly associated with childhood maltreatment. Thus, although primary and secondary prevention remain important approaches, tertiary prevention may be critically important. Many tertiary prevention strategies involve new approaches based on **restorative justice** principles. Restorative justice attempts to personalize crimes by having victims and offenders mediate restitution agreements which are satisfactory to each. Restorative justice contrasts more punitive approaches based on retributive justice which satisfies legal requirements based on punishment.

In restorative justice, victims take an active role in the process while offenders take meaningful responsibility for their actions and attempt to right their wrongs. Additionally, restorative justice aims to help perpetrators to avoid future offenses.

Test-Taking Strategies Applied

The question requires knowledge about the characteristics of perpetrators, as well as tertiary prevention. Tertiary refers to treatment of clients with identified conditions. The goal of tertiary prevention is to minimize further damage. While the incorrect answers are accurate statements, they do not help reduce child abuse. Treating victims will assist with dealing with the effects of the abuse, reducing the likelihood that they will be abusers themselves.

Knowledge Area

Unit II—Assessment (Content Area); Concepts of Abuse and Neglect (Competency); The Characteristics of Perpetrators of Abuse, Neglect, and Exploitation (KSA)

132. B

Rationale

Compassion fatigue, also used interchangeably in the literature with secondary traumatic stress and vicarious trauma, is best defined as a syndrome consisting of a combination of the symptoms of secondary traumatic stress and professional burnout. Compassion fatigue recently emerged in the literature as a more general term describing the overall experience of emotional and physical fatigue that social service professionals experience due to the chronic use of empathy when treating clients who are suffering in some way. The chronic use of empathy combined with the day-to-day bureaucratic hurdles that exist for many social workers, such as agency stress, billing difficulties, and balancing clinical work with administrative work, generate compassion fatigue. Much like professional burnout, the experience of compassion fatigue tends to occur cumulatively over time, whereas vicarious trauma and secondary traumatic stress have more immediate onset. For those who treat victims of trauma, secondary traumatic stress may contribute to the overall experience of compassion fatigue; however, those who treat populations other than trauma victims may also experience compassion fatigue without experiencing secondary traumatic stress.

Test-Taking Strategies Applied

The question contains a qualifying word—BEST. Although parts of the incorrect response choices, such as physical exhaustion, may result from compassion fatigue, none of the other answers are optimal in their entirety. Social workers do not have to work long hours in dangerous situations to get compassion fatigue. In addition, it may not result in a psychological problem and is not a psychosomatic attempt at getting compassion from others.

Knowledge Area

Unit IV—Professional Relationships, Values, and Ethics (Content Area); Professional Development and Use of Self (Competency); Burnout, Secondary Trauma, and Compassion Fatigue (KSA)

133. B

Rationale

The **nature versus nurture** debate focuses on the relative importance of biological (genes, heredity, etc.) and environmental factors on human development. Some highlight that nature has a significant influence on growth, from physical appearance to personality characteristics.

Others refer to environmental variables, such as early childhood experiences, social relationships, and the surrounding culture, as nurturing or inhibiting development.

Some of the incorrect answers are based on other debates, but not the one that is the focus of the question.

Determinism suggests that only one course of events is possible, whereas **free will** is the ability to choose between different possible courses of action.

The dispute between **rationalism** and **empiricism** concerns the extent to which knowledge acquisition is dependent upon sense experience. Rationalists claim that there are significant ways in which concepts and knowledge are gained independently of sense experience. Empiricists claim that sense experience is the ultimate source of all our concepts and knowledge.

Test-Taking Strategies Applied

This is a recall question that relies on social workers understanding the major debate of whether growth is mainly determined by a client's innate qualities (nature) or by his or her personal experiences (nurture). However, social workers recognize that this is a false dichotomy as there is overwhelming evidence that, from the earliest points in development, gene activity interacts with events and experiences in the environment.

Knowledge Area

Unit I—Human Development, Diversity, and Behavior in the Environment (Content Area); Human Growth and Development (Competency); Theories of Human Development Throughout the Lifespan (e.g., Physical, Social, Emotional, Cognitive, Behavioral) (KSA)

134. C

Rationale

Recurrent substance-related legal problems (e.g., arrests for substance-related disorderly conduct) were removed from the *DSM-5*. Its removal was justified as it did not add diagnostic assistance. Clients who have recurrent legal problems as a result of their **drug use** nearly always meet other criteria (e.g., drug use in physically hazardous situations such as driving, failure to fulfill major role obligations, or recurrent social or interpersonal problems).

In addition, legal involvement is related to race and economic factors, with people of color more likely to be arrested and to receive harsher punishments for their alleged crimes. Thus, legal problems are not good indicators of substance use issues because they are more closely linked to other factors, and those with substance use problems are likely to meet other diagnostic criteria.

Test-Taking Strategies Applied

The question contains a qualifying word—PRIMARY—that indicates that there may be more than one valid reason for not using recurrent substance-related legal problems as a diagnostic criterion. Several of the response choices are accurate statements. However, the main reason that it is not a sound indicator of the presence of a substance use issue is that it is more closely related to race and economic factors than the severity of the problem.

Knowledge Area

Unit II—Assessment (Content Area); Assessment Methods and Techniques (Competency); The Diagnostic and Statistical Manual of the American Psychiatric Association (KSA)

135. B

Rationale

Intellectual Disability (Intellectual Developmental Disorder), formerly known as Mental Retardation, includes intellectual deficits and difficulty functioning in daily life in areas such as communication, self-care, housekeeping, social/interpersonal skills, self-direction, academics, work, leisure, health, and safety. Its onset is during the developmental period. Intellectual disability has many different etiologies. Prior to the publication of *DSM-5* in 2013, diagnostic criteria for Mental Retardation required an IQ score of 70 or below. In the *DSM-5*, IQ scores have been deemphasized. There is no longer a cutoff score or threshold per se for establishing a diagnosis. Rather, scaled IQ scores are evaluated in context with a client's entire clinical picture.

Test-Taking Strategies Applied

This is a recall question that relies on social workers understanding the symptoms of mental and emotional illness across the lifespan. Mental Retardation is a term that is no longer accepted in the field; intellectual disabilities should be used in its place. Understanding that Mental Retardation was related to cognitive impairment can assist in selecting the correct answer, because Intellectual Developmental Disorder is the only one that refers to intelligence specifically.

Knowledge Area

Unit II—Assessment (Content Area); Assessment Methods and Techniques (Competency); The Diagnostic and Statistical Manual of the American Psychiatric Association (KSA)

136. C

Rationale

Case conferences are often used to understand and solve complex client situations. Today, case conferences are often done remotely instead of face-to-face. They involve social workers and others (including the client, members of the client's family, other professionals, etc.) coming together to discuss issues or plans for the future.

Test-Taking Strategies Applied

The question requires the correct answer to be distinguished from the incorrect ones, as it must assist the social worker to "most effectively understand the current situation." Speaking with the teachers to determine whether homework can be done in school may be helpful, but it does not aid in understanding or assessing the problems. Using school records and examining the client's academic history will not provide a full understanding of issues facing the family that may account for the client's poor academic performance.

Case conferencing is the best method for hearing the challenges directly from the client and her family. Having her teachers present for the meeting will give them insight into the difficulties being experienced and can lead to creative problem solving based on the ideas of all parties.

Knowledge Area

Unit II—Assessment (Content Area); Assessment Methods and Techniques (Competency); Methods of Involving Clients/Client Systems in Problem Identification (e.g., Gathering Collateral Information) (KSA)

137. A

Rationale

According to the *NASW Code of Ethics*, social workers should inform clients, to the extent possible, about the **disclosure of confidential information** and the potential consequences—when feasible, before the disclosure is made. This applies whether social workers disclose confidential information on the basis of a legal requirement or client consent (*NASW Code of Ethics, 2008—1.07 Privacy and Confidentiality*).

Test-Taking Strategies Applied

This is a recall question that relies on social workers understanding the ethical standards related to releasing confidential information as required by court orders. Simply sending copies of court orders to clients is not sufficient as they may not be aware of the information that is to be released and the consequences of the disclosures. Clients should always be made aware of disclosures, although it is recognized that it may sometimes not be feasible to make such notifications before disclosures are made. In these circumstances, notifications should be made as soon as possible. Although social workers may want to seek legal advice from attorneys, it is not required and is not the correct response choice—such actions do not put the client's interests first.

Knowledge Area

Unit IV—Professional Relationships, Values, and Ethics (Content Area); Confidentiality (Competency); Legal and/or Ethical Issues Regarding Confidentiality, Including Electronic Information Security (KSA)

138. D

Rationale

Collectivistic cultures emphasize the needs and goals of the group as a whole over the needs and wishes of each individual. In such cultures, relationships with other members of the group and the interconnectedness between people play a central role in each person's identity. Cultures in Asia, Central America, South America, and Africa tend to be more collectivistic. A few common traits of collectivistic cultures include:

- Focusing on promoting selflessness and putting the community needs ahead of individual needs
- Working as a group and supporting others
- Encouraging members to do what is best for society
- Viewing families and communities as having central roles

In collectivistic cultures, people are considered "good" if they are generous, helpful, dependable, and attentive to the needs of others. This contrasts with individualistic cultures that often place a greater emphasis on characteristics such as assertiveness and independence.

Test-Taking Strategies Applied

The question contains a qualifying word—NOT—that requires social workers to select the response choice that is not valued in collectivistic cultures. When NOT is used as a qualifying word, it is often helpful to remove it from the question and eliminate the three response choices that are valued in collectivistic cultures. This approach will leave the one response choice that is NOT valued.

Even if there is little knowledge about collectivistic cultures, the correct answer may be evident. "Collect" means to gather together, so it is possible to assume that collectivistic cultures value groups. Independence is the one response choice that appears antithetical to this orientation.

Knowledge Area

Unit I—Human Development, Diversity, and Behavior in the Environment (Content Area); Diversity, Social/Economic Justice, and Oppression (Competency); The Effect of Culture, Race, and Ethnicity on Behaviors, Attitudes, and Identity (KSA)

139. B

Rationale

Gender identity is the innermost concept of self as male, female, both, or neither, depending on how clients perceive themselves and what they call themselves. A client's gender identity can be the same or different than the gender assigned at birth. Most people develop a gender identity that matches their biological gender. For some, however, their gender identity is different from their biological or assigned gender. Some choose to socially, hormonally, and/or surgically change their biological gender to more fully match their gender identity.

Gender identity has to be determined through speaking with a client because it is based on the client's perception. It is not in records or tests. It also may be different than that which is evident, so observations will not be helpful.

Test-Taking Strategies Applied

The question contains a qualifying word—best—though it is not capitalized. Identity is the conception, qualities, beliefs, and expressions that make a person distinct from others. While gender expression may be evident from physical observation, the beliefs that a client holds will only be revealed through questioning. Gender expression and gender identity may not be congruent, so observations may be misleading.

Knowledge Area

Unit I—Human Development, Diversity, and Behavior in the Environment (Content Area); Diversity, Social/Economic Justice, and Oppression (Competency); Gender and Gender Identity Concepts (KSA)

140. C

Rationale

Social workers are **mandatory reporters** of abuse. It is not the social worker's responsibility to determine if the child is at continued risk.

The child protection agency—which has different names in each state—is the expert in investigating these suspicions. The social worker should not delay the report to get additional information or monitor the situation. The case scenario begins with an assertion that the social worker believes that physical abuse is occurring, which should prompt an immediate report to the child protection agency.

Test-Taking Strategies Applied

Although some agencies may have protocols that require supervisory notification, or a social worker may feel it necessary to also inform his or her supervisor about the need to report, these factors vary from situation to situation or agency to agency. There is no ethical mandate to speak to a supervisor in this situation. This question aims to test whether a social worker will delay reporting for any reason (including gathering more information or seeking supervision) or get involved in the investigation (by definitively proving that it occurred). Delays should not occur and social workers should be familiar with signs of child abuse so they are capable of making a mandatory report when they are present.

Knowledge Area

Unit IV—Professional Relationships, Values, and Ethics (Content Area); Professional Values and Ethical Issues (Competency); Legal and/or Ethical Issues Regarding Mandatory Reporting (e.g., Abuse, Threat of Harm, Impaired Professionals, etc.) (KSA)

141. A

Rationale

Group work is a method of serving people in groups for personal growth, the enhancement of social functioning, and for the achievement of socially desirable goals. One factor affecting group cohesion is group size. It is posited that groups larger than six members will produce lower trust, cohesion, and commitment than those smaller than six members. Group size is linked to these processes through the mechanism of anticipated mutual perception or the amount an individual considers what others in the group are thinking about him or her.

Group members also have more "buy in" or cohesion if they participate in goal and norm setting. Closed groups are those in which designated individuals meet for a predetermined length of time. They have greater cohesion than open groups in which individuals can enter and leave at will.

Homogeneity, or similarity of group members—not heterogeneity—increases cohesion.

Test-Taking Strategies Applied

The question contains a qualifying word—NOT—that requires social workers to select the response choice that is not likely to increase cohesion. When NOT is used as a qualifying word, it is often helpful to remove it from the question and eliminate the three response choices that are essential to increased cohesion. This approach will leave the one response choice that is NOT likely to increase solidarity between group members.

Knowledge Area

Unit I—Human Development, Diversity, and Behavior in the Environment (Content Area); Human Behavior in the Social Environment (Competency); Theories of Group Development and Functioning (KSA)

142. B

Rationale

Motor skills greatly vary depending on the proper functioning of the brain, joints, skeleton, and, most especially, the nervous system. Motor skills are subdivided into two kinds, namely gross motor skills and fine motor skills. Gross motor skills are the skills learned and acquired until early childhood. Gross movements come from a huge group of muscles and entire body movement. Fine motor skills pertain to the coordination of muscle movements in the body, such as the eyes, toes, and fingers. They allow one to write, grasp small objects, and fasten clothing.

To assess gross motor skills, clients may be asked to crawl, stand, and walk, as well as throw, catch, and kick a ball. Fine motor skills are assessed through picking up objects such as buttons, straws, marbles, and blocks and placing them in mugs, jars, boxes, and cups or by stacking blocks, opening jars, buttoning, and tying laces.

Test-Taking Strategies Applied

The question contains a qualifying word—MOST. Although this task may be part of a battery of activities to assess other areas of development, such as cognition, it is likely related to fine motor control. It does not relate to assessment of social skills or expressive communication, which is the ability to communicate with others. The task may relate to receptive language that is the ability to listen and understand, but it is not a response choice listed.

Knowledge Area

Unit II—Assessment (Content Area); Assessment Methods and Techniques (Competency); Techniques and Instruments Used to Assess Clients/Client Systems (KSA)

143. A

Rationale

Developmental disabilities, an umbrella term, include intellectual disability as well as other disabilities that are apparent during childhood. Developmental disabilities are severe, chronic disabilities that can be cognitive or physical, or both. The disabilities appear before the age of 22 and are likely to be lifelong. Some developmental disabilities are largely physical issues, such as cerebral palsy or epilepsy. Some individuals may have a condition that includes a physical and intellectual disability, such as Down syndrome. The evaluation and classification of intellectual disability is a complex issue. There are three major criteria for intellectual disability: significant limitations in intellectual functioning, significant limitations in adaptive behavior, and onset in childhood. An intelligence test is a major tool in measuring intellectual functioning, which is the mental capacity for learning, reasoning, problem solving, and so on. The Wechsler Intelligence Scale is a very popular intelligence test.

Test-Taking Strategies Applied

The question contains a qualifying word—MOST. Although Down syndrome can be comorbid with other conditions, there is no indication in the case scenario that other issues exist. Thus, a test of intelligence is likely to be in the student's record because Down syndrome is a cognitive disability.

Knowledge Area

Unit II—Assessment (Content Area); Assessment Methods and Techniques (Competency); Techniques and Instruments Used to Assess Clients/Client Systems (KSA)

144. B

Rationale

Malingering is **feigning illness** or grossly exaggerated physical or psychological complaints with the goal of receiving a reward, including, but not limited to, money, medications, avoidance of punishment/ work, and so on. Malingering is not a psychiatric disorder and can lead to abuse of the medical system, with unnecessary tests being performed and time taken away from other patients.

Malingering can exist in a variety of intensities, from pure (in which all symptoms are falsified) to partial, in which symptoms are exaggerated. Malingering is not easy to detect as symptoms are often self-reported. In addition, it is hard to gather data, especially if the client has some symptoms of a physical disorder but is just exaggerating them.

Malingering should not be confused with Factitious Disorder (in which the motive is the desire to occupy a sick role, rather than some form of material gain) and Somatic Symptom Disorder (in which symptoms are not produced willfully).

Test-Taking Strategies Applied

This is a recall question that relies on social workers understanding disorders and key terms associated with feigning illness. The correct answer gets to the reasoning behind the behavior—reward—as the gain reinforces client claims. Often maladaptive behaviors are reinforced, causing them to be sustained and/or increased. It is important to distinguish malingering from Factitious Disorder in which clients' motivation is to take on a sick role, evoking sympathy and attention.

Knowledge Area

Unit II—Assessment (Content Area); Assessment Methods and Techniques (Competency); The Indicators of Feigning Illness (KSA)

145. A

Rationale

The importance of using **interdisciplinary team approaches** is becoming increasingly recognized. Social workers serve on teams with medical professionals, teachers, police officers, probation officers, attorneys, and so on. To practice effectively, social workers must be prepared to work with all individuals in clients' environments.

A challenge is that each profession has a different culture that includes values, beliefs, attitudes, customs, and behaviors. Professional cultures evolved as the different professions developed, reflecting historic factors as well as social class and gender issues. Educational experiences and the socialization process that occurs during the training of each professional reinforce common values, problem-solving approaches, and language/jargon. Personal and professional cultural differences can lead to conflict among members, challenging effective interdisciplinary teamwork. Insight into educational, systemic, and personal factors that contribute to culture can help guide social workers to better understand viewpoints, communication styles, and values of team members. Such insight is useful in negotiating successful resolution of conflicts needed for collaborative practice.

Test-Taking Strategies Applied

The question contains a qualifying word—MOST. Although the incorrect response choices are true statements, they do not address the most challenging aspect of interdisciplinary team approaches—cultural differences. Collaboration is a skill that requires attention and practice. If social workers do not recognize differences in work style, communication, and beliefs to personal and professional values, they may be apt to blame other team members for conflicts that arise.

Knowledge Area

Unit III—Interventions With Clients/Client Systems (Content Area); Use of Collaborative Relationships (Competency); The Process of Interdisciplinary and Intradisciplinary Team Collaboration (KSA)

146. B

Rationale

Respite care provides temporary relief to those who are **caregiving** for family members who might otherwise require permanent placement in facilities outside their homes. Respite programs provide planned, short-term and time-limited breaks for families and other unpaid caregivers of children and adults with disabilities and illnesses in order *to support and maintain primary caregiving relationships.*

Respite has been shown to help sustain family caregiver health and well-being, avoid or delay out-of-home placements, and reduce the likelihood of abuse and neglect. Health and well-being of family caregivers can be compromised because of their responsibilities. Respite care is a chance for them to take a break. Respite is the service most often requested by family caregivers.

Test-Taking Strategies Applied

The question contains a qualifying word—NOT—that requires social workers to select the response choice that does not justify the provision of respite. All of the response choices are true statements, but only one is correct as it does not directly relate to the reasons for respite care. The incorrect answers include information about parental well-being impacting on children, parental caregiving being optimal for children, and the stress associated with raising children with developmental disabilities. These statements support the need to give breaks to parents who may be experiencing increased stress due to their caregiving responsibilities. Although early intervention is important, it is not associated with caregiving, which is at the heart of respite services.

Knowledge Area

Unit III—Interventions With Clients/Client Systems (Content Area); Indicators and Effects of Crisis and Change (Competency); The Impact of Caregiving on Families (KSA)

147. B

Rationale

A client is the source of essential information through which to define problems and solutions. A client is an expert in his or her own life situation. The **problem-solving process** contains the following steps: engagement, assessment, planning, intervention, evaluation, and termination. However, this process is fluid, with a social worker needing to readily move between these steps as the helping relationship unfolds. *Assessment is not a discrete task, but continuous during the entire process.* A client provides insight into the presenting problem, as well as his or her strengths and challenges, throughout the helping relationship. A social worker should be collecting information, even if only informally, to assess the situation, starting with the initial interaction in the first meeting.

Test-Taking Strategies Applied

This is a recall question that relies on social workers understanding the steps in the problem-solving process. This process must be adapted to the individual circumstances that can affect the building and maintaining of the helping relationship. Social workers must be flexible in their approaches and the correct answer is the only one that does not limit assessment as occurring at a single specific time in the process.

Knowledge Area

Unit II—Assessment (Content Area); Assessment Methods and Techniques (Competency); Methods of Involving Clients/Client Systems in Problem Identification (e.g., Gathering Collateral Information) (KSA)

148. B

Rationale

Relapse is generally considered to be the return to substance use after a period of abstinence. Relapse occurs because an addictive disorder is a chronic disorder. As there is no cure, there is always the potential for relapse. Addiction is a chronic illness, and like any other chronic illness, it must be managed over time. There are many risk factors for relapse, including a powerful need to stimulate reward centers within the brain. Both external and internal factors can create the urge to use drugs or alcohol again. Internal risk factors include a persistently negative mood, feeling stressed or depressed, a genetic predisposition to or family history of addiction, and/or coexisting psychiatric problems such as Attention-Deficit/Hyperactivity Disorder, depression, and anxiety.

In the case scenario, the client is discussing the struggles, indicating a need for help from the social worker. Help seeking is important after relapse. It is clear that the client has a desire to maintain sobriety due to being upset about the recent relapse. The "immediate goal" needs to be getting the client access to supports, such as self-help groups or other treatment options that promote abstinence.

Test-Taking Strategies Applied

The question asks for "the immediate goal." Although identifying the external and internal triggers is important, the most pressing issue is staying sober and getting the resources (e.g., support) to do so. The client's commitment should be focused on the immediate goal of making it through 24 hours without using again. After 24 hours, another 24-hour commitment can be made. Long-term commitments can be overwhelming for the client. Relapses do not mean that the client has lost everything learned about addiction and recovery. The client will need to work through the shame that often accompanies relapse, but the "immediate goal" is to stand on solid ground in recovery again.

Knowledge Area

Unit I—Human Development, Diversity, and Behavior in the Environment (Content Area); Human Behavior in the Social Environment (Competency); Addiction Theories and Concepts (KSA)

149. C

Rationale

When receiving **a subpoena**, a social worker should respond and claim privilege but should not turn over records or any other client information—including a summary as described in the case scenario— unless the court issues a subsequent order to do so. *A subpoena and court order are not the same.* When a social worker gets a court order, he or she should try to limit its scope and/or ask that the records be sealed. This same standard applies to both current and past clients, living or dead.

Test-Taking Strategies Applied

This is a recall question that relies on social workers understanding the legal issues regarding confidentiality, and specifically what to do when receiving a subpoena or court order. The use of a former client—instead of a current one—in the case scenario does not alter the social worker's mandate. It is important to understand that a subpoena is a request by the court for information and that the social worker must not release it, claiming privilege, until court ordered to do so.

Knowledge Area

Unit IV—Professional Relationships, Values, and Ethics (Content Area); Confidentiality (Competency); Legal and/or Ethical Issues Regarding Confidentiality, Including Electronic Information Security (KSA)

150. D

Rationale

In instances when **clients lack the capacity to provide informed consent**, social workers should protect clients' interests by seeking permission from appropriate third parties, informing clients consistent with their levels of understanding. In such instances, social workers should seek to ensure that the third parties act in a manner consistent with the clients' wishes and interests and should take reasonable steps to safeguard their rights.

Deciding whether clients are legally competent to make decisions regarding their own treatment requires assessments of their mental capacity. Competency evaluations are usually done by professionals who have been properly trained in conducting them. In addition, ultimately courts will need to be involved and weigh the information presented to determine legal competency. Social workers cannot determine whether clients' legal rights to make decisions can be limited. However, they can and should advocate with the courts to regain clients' rights in instances where clients have been found to be legally incompetent and, in the social workers' professional opinion, they are able to make sound decisions.

Test-Taking Strategies Applied

The question contains a qualifying word—NOT—that requires social workers to select the response choice that is not required by the professional code of ethics when working with clients who lack the capacity to provide informed consent. When NOT is used as a qualifying word, it is often helpful to remove it from the question and eliminate the three response choices that are essential. This approach will leave the one response choice that is NOT required.

Knowledge Area

Unit IV—Professional Relationships, Values, and Ethics (Content Area); Confidentiality (Competency); The Principles and Processes of Obtaining Informed Consent (KSA)

151. A

Rationale

Various forms of **hallucination** exist, with some involving voices that can be heard and others involving nonexistent smells or tastes. Hallucinations are a common symptom of Schizophrenia, but they can also be caused by drug abuse or excessive alcohol intake, fever, bereavement, depression, or dementia. Auditory hallucinations are the most common form of hallucination in those with Schizophrenia and refer to the perception of nonexistent sounds. Visual hallucinations are when something is seen that does not exist. Olfactory hallucinations involve smelling odors that do not exist; these odors are usually unpleasant, such as vomit, urine, feces, smoke, or rotting flesh.

Tactile hallucinations refer to when a client senses that he or she is being touched when he or she is not being touched.

Test-Taking Strategies Applied

The question contains a qualifying word—MOST. While a client with Schizophrenia may experience other types of hallucinations, the client probably is hearing nonexistent sounds or voices as these are the most prevalent type.

Knowledge Area

Unit II—Assessment (Content Area); Biopsychosocial History and Collateral Data (Competency); The Indicators of Mental and Emotional Illness Throughout the Lifespan (KSA)

152. A

Rationale

The term **cycle of abuse** refers to repeated and dangerous acts of violence as a cyclical pattern. The pattern, or cycle, repeats and can happen many times during a relationship. Each phase may last a different length of time, and over time the level of violence may increase. The first phase is tension building, followed by the second, battering. Violence results in a "honeymoon" or period of contrition (remorse). However, the phases—tension-building, battering, and honeymoon—may occur in any order.

In relationships marked by violence, it is likely additional battering will continue and there is grave danger in leaving an abuser at any time, making the other response choices incorrect.

Test-Taking Strategies Applied

The correct response choice should be selected "based on the cycle of abuse." The case scenario describes a battering incident followed by a honeymoon. Thus, a period of tension building would be expected before more violence follows.

Knowledge Area

Unit III—Interventions With Clients/Client Systems (Content Area); Intervention Processes and Techniques (Competency); The Impact of Domestic, Intimate Partner, and Other Violence on the Helping Relationship (KSA)

153. C

Rationale

Group services provide benefits that individual services may not. Group members are almost always surprised by how rewarding the group experience can be. *Groups act as a support network and "sounding board."* Other members of the group often help with specific ideas for improving a difficult situation or life challenge, holding members accountable along the way. Regularly talking and listening to others also helps clients put their own problems in perspective. Many clients experience difficulties, but few speak openly about them to those they do not know well. Often, clients feel like they are the only ones struggling—but they are not. It can be a relief to hear others discuss what they are going through. Diversity of experiences is another important benefit of group services. By seeing how others tackle problems and make positive changes, clients can discover a whole range of strategies for facing their concerns.

Test-Taking Strategies Applied

The question contains a qualifying word—PRIMARY—that indicates that group services may have more than one of the benefits listed, but the main benefit must be selected from the rest. Comparing group to individual services highlights the main benefit—peer support. Hearing from others who may be experiencing similar problems reduces isolation and helps clients learn from their successes and mistakes.

Knowledge Area

Unit III—Interventions With Clients/Client Systems (Content Area); Intervention Processes and Techniques (Competency); The Criteria Used in the Selection of Intervention/Treatment Modalities (e.g., Client/Client System Abilities, Culture, Life Stage) (KSA)

154. A

Rationale

The prefix *cis-* is Latin meaning "on this side of," whereas *trans-* means "on the other side of." **Cisgender** is a word that applies to the vast majority of people, describing those who are not transgender or whose gender identities conform to that assigned at birth. In 2013, Oxford Dictionaries added "cisgender" as a term. It recognizes that all people have gender identities, even if they are not challenged or questioned.

Test-Taking Strategies Applied

This is a recall question that relies on social workers' understanding of terms associated with gender identity.

Knowledge Area

Unit I—Human Development, Diversity, and Behavior in the Environment (Content Area); Diversity, Social/Economic Justice, and Oppression (Competency); Gender and Gender Identity Concepts (KSA)

155. D

Rationale

In this case scenario, the client's fears appear to be based on a lack of information about the procedure. **Electroencephalography**, or EEG, monitors brain activity through the skull. EEG is used to help diagnose certain seizure disorders, brain tumors, brain damage from head injuries, inflammation of the brain and/or spinal cord, alcoholism, certain psychiatric disorders, and metabolic and degenerative disorders that affect the brain. EEGs are also used to evaluate sleep disorders, monitor brain activity when a client has been fully anesthetized or has lost consciousness, and confirm brain death.

This painless, risk-free test can be performed in a doctor's office, hospital, or testing facility. A series of cup-like electrodes are attached to the scalp, either with a special conducting paste or with extremely fine needles. The electrodes (also called leads) are small devices that are attached to wires and carry the electrical energy of the brain to a machine for reading. A very low electrical current is sent through the electrodes and the baseline brain energy is recorded. Clients are then exposed to a variety of external stimuli—including bright or flashing light, noise, or certain drugs—or are asked to open and close their eyes or to change breathing patterns. The electrodes transmit the resulting changes in brain wave patterns. Since movement and nervousness can change brain wave patterns, clients usually recline in a chair or on a bed during the test, which takes up to an hour. Testing for certain disorders requires performing an EEG during sleep, which takes at least 3 hours.

Test-Taking Strategies Applied

The question contains a qualifying word—BEST. Although some of the response choices may be useful, the most appropriate way to address client fears due to a lack of information or misinformation is through education. The client's fear of needles and low tolerance for pain can be addressed by understanding more about the procedure, which is usually not invasive or painful.

Knowledge Area

Unit II—Assessment (Content Area); Biopsychosocial History and Collateral Data (Competency); Basic Medical Terminology (KSA)

156. D

Rationale

In micro practice, social workers must work with clients to identify the problems to be addressed. **Problem identification** concerns determining the problem targeted for intervention. Although this seems straightforward, it is often difficult to isolate the issue that, when addressed, will result in a change in the symptomology of a client.

In this case scenario, the client's anxiety is instigated by some thought, behavior, or circumstance. Finding out what is causing this distress is essential to solving the problem. Understanding what the client is experiencing before the anxiety starts (the antecedents) and how often it occurs (the frequency) is essential to problem formulation. Anxiety may be caused by many factors, and until the precursors are identified it is impossible to attempt to eradicate or mitigate the source.

Test-Taking Strategies Applied

The case scenario states that the client "does not know what is causing" her episodes of anxiety. Determining the etiology must be the focus in order to meet the client's need of addressing her anxiety. Although several of the response choices may be helpful, only the correct answer directly relates to her episodes. Collecting family history, collateral information, and information on the client's coping skills may shed no light on the thoughts, behaviors, or circumstances that trigger the anxiety. Without knowing its cause, it is not possible to try to treat it.

Knowledge Area

Unit II—Assessment (Content Area); Assessment Methods and Techniques (Competency); The Factors and Processes Used in Problem Formulation (KSA)

157. B

Rationale

Although the question does not refer to **Maslow's hierarchy of needs**, knowledge of his model is required. Maslow described five motivational needs, often depicted as a hierarchical pyramid. The five-stage model can be divided into deficiency (basic) needs (physiological, safety, love, and esteem) and growth needs (self-actualization).

The deficiency, or basic, needs are said to motivate people when they are unmet. Also, the need to fulfill them will become stronger the longer that they are denied.

Clients must satisfy lower level basic needs before meeting higher level growth needs.

Every person has the desire to move up the hierarchy toward a level of self-actualization, but not all are able to do so.

Test-Taking Strategies Applied

The question contains a qualifying word—NOT—that requires social workers to select the response choice which is not a deficiency need. When NOT is used as a qualifying word, it is often helpful to remove it from the question and eliminate the three response choices that are deficiency needs. This approach will leave the one response choice that is NOT a deficiency need. Deficiency needs are more basic, so it may help to assess each response choice with regard to how essential it is for survival or simple well-being.

Knowledge Area

Unit I—Human Development, Diversity, and Behavior in the Environment (Content Area); Human Growth and Development (Competency); Basic Human Needs (KSA)

158. C

Rationale

In this case scenario, the social worker's actions are unethical for many reasons. First, the social worker is taking unfair advantage of her professional relationship by purchasing the client's home for "far less than its assessed value." This promotion of a business interest is prohibited by the *NASW Code of Ethics*. Second, agreeing to rent the home to the client creates a **dual or multiple relationship**. A conflict of interest occurs when a social worker relates to a client in more than one relationship, such as landlord–tenant. The social worker should have been alerted to and avoided this conflict of interest.

Test-Taking Strategies Applied

This is a recall question that relies on social workers' understanding of ethical standards related to conflicts of interest. The *NASW Code of Ethics* can assist if such conflicts arise. The need for social workers to avoid conflicts of interest whenever possible is clear.

Knowledge Area

Unit IV—Professional Relationships, Values, and Ethics (Content Area); Professional Values and Ethical Issues (Competency); Ethical Issues Related to Dual Relationships (KSA)

159. A

Rationale

Equifinality refers to the concept that similar outcomes may stem from different early experiences. For example, different early experiences in life (e.g., parental divorce, physical abuse, parental substance abuse) can lead to similar outcomes, such as the presence of a mental health disorder. The same ends can be achieved by many different means or ways.

Throughput is energy that is integrated by a system that can be used by the system to accomplish its goals.

Entropy is a closed, disorganized, stagnant system that depletes available energy.

Homeostasis is a steady state within a system.

Test-Taking Strategies Applied

This is a recall question that relies on social workers understanding systems theory. When studying theories, models, and perspectives, it is essential to not only understand the overarching concepts, but also the terms associated with them. This question does not mention systems theory, but it is asking for the definition of a term associated with it. All the answers are terms that are germane to this perspective. Thus, knowing terms can be as important as being familiar with theories, models, or perspectives themselves in answering questions correctly.

Knowledge Area

Unit I—Human Development, Diversity, and Behavior in the Environment (Content Area); Human Behavior in the Social Environment (Competency); Systems and Ecological Perspectives and Theories (KSA)

160. A

Rationale

A social worker's ethical responsibility as a professional includes preventing and addressing impairment. According to the *NASW Code of Ethics*, social workers should not allow their own personal problems, psychosocial distress, legal problems, substance abuse, or mental health difficulties to interfere with their professional judgment and performance or to jeopardize the best interests of people for whom they have a professional responsibility.

Burnout can easily occur in social work practice. There are many symptoms associated with burnout including confusion; impaired judgment and decision making; forgetfulness; and decreased ability to identify alternatives, prioritize tasks, and evaluate one's own performance. Thus, the social worker in the case scenario is not equipped to identify the causes of her burnout and/or monitor the situation.

In order "to appropriately deal with this situation," as required by the question, the social worker must take action. Consulting with a supervisor to have him or her determine the need for intervention is not enough. The social worker should immediately take appropriate remedial action by seeking professional help, making adjustments in workload, terminating practice, or taking any other steps necessary to protect clients and others.

Test-Taking Strategies Applied

The correct answer must "appropriately deal with this situation." Several of the response choices do not involve taking action or dealing with the problem. Therefore, they should be eliminated. Only one, the correct response, definitely describes steps to be taken to minimize impact to clients, which is always a top priority for social workers.

Knowledge Area

Unit IV—Professional Relationships, Values, and Ethics (Content Area); Professional Development and Use of Self (Competency); Social Worker Self-Care Principles and Techniques (KSA)

161. C

Rationale

There are many myths about childhood sexual abuse. Victims often fail to disclose their abuse in a timely fashion. This delay is frequently used as evidence that an alleged victim's story should be doubted. However, research shows that children who have been sexually assaulted often have considerable difficulty in revealing or discussing their abuse.

One of the most dangerous assumptions is the belief that adults who appear both educated and financially successful could not be child molesters. Sex offenders are well aware of the propensity for making assumptions about private behavior from one's public presentation, and they use this information to gain access to child victims.

A lack of physical evidence of sexual assault is often cited as support that an alleged perpetrator must be innocent. However, research shows that abnormal genital findings are rare, even in cases where the abuse has been proven. Some acts, like fondling and oral sex, leave no physical traces. Even injuries from penetration heal very quickly in young children, so abnormal genital findings are not common, especially if the child is examined more than 48 hours after the abuse.

It is true that not everyone who comes in contact with a child molester will be abused. Although this finding may seem obvious, some interpret the fact that abusers did not molest particular children in their care to mean that those children who do allege abuse must be lying. In truth, sex offenders tend to carefully pick and set up their victims. Thus, while sex offenders may feel driven to molest children, they rarely do so indiscriminately.

Test-Taking Strategies Applied

The question contains a qualifying word—TRUE. It is even capitalized to assist with identifying the distinguishing factor of the correct response from the rest. Each statement must be read carefully and evaluated as to its accuracy. The correct answer is identified through a process of elimination, with each false assertion being excluded.

Knowledge Area

Unit II—Assessment (Content Area); Concepts of Abuse and Neglect (Competency); Indicators and Dynamics of Abuse and Neglect Throughout the Lifespan (KSA)

162. A

Rationale

The **strengths perspective** identifies the inherent strengths of clients and builds on them. It is about finding good even in the worst situation. It avoids the use of stigmatizing language or terminology, which clients use on themselves and eventually identify with, accept, and feel helpless to change. It fosters hope by focusing on what is or has been historically successful for clients.

The **feminist perspective** takes into account the role of gender and the historical lack of power experienced by women in our society. It focuses on equality and empowerment of women in our society.

The **conflict perspective** typically looks for sources of conflict and causes of human behavior in the economic and political arenas, and more recently in the cultural arena. It is based on the belief that groups and individuals try to advance their own interests over the interests of others as they compete for scarce resources.

The **rational choice perspective** sees human behavior as based on self-interest and rational choices about effective ways to accomplish goals. Human interaction is seen as an exchange of resources, and clients make judgments about the fairness of the exchange (social exchange theory).

Test-Taking Strategies Applied

This is a recall question that relies on social workers understanding various practice perspectives. Using a strengths-based approach is essential to client empowerment. Clients should not be blamed for their problems, and there are always characteristics such as resilience and the ability to seek help that can be viewed as strengths, even in crisis situations.

Knowledge Area

Unit II—Assessment (Content Area); Assessment Methods and Techniques (Competency); Methods to Assess the Client's/Client System's Strengths, Resources, and Challenges (e.g., Individual, Family, Group, Organization, Community) (KSA)

163. C

Rationale

Social workers focus on assisting clients to **identify problems** and areas of strength, as well as increasing problem-solving strategies. It is essential that, throughout the problem-solving process, social workers view clients as experts in their lives. Clients should be asked what they would like to see changed in their lives and clients' definitions of problems should be accepted. Clients should be asked what will be different in their lives when their problems are solved. Social workers should listen carefully for, and work hard to respect, the directions in which clients want to go with their lives (their goals) and the words they use to express these directions.

Clients should be asked about the paths that they would like to take to make desired changes. Clients' perceptions should be respected and clients' inner resources (strengths) should be maximized as part of treatment. A social worker should also make sure that the needs are based on an unbiased assessment and client wishes. They should not be driven by funding and time constraints.

Social workers should not recommend only services that are familiar or provided by their employing agencies—this would be a "cookie cutter" or "one size fits all" approach.

Test-Taking Strategies Applied

The question focuses on social work services for "the same client system need in the same setting." Although the incorrect response choices are concerns in any setting, they are not more prevalent under these conditions. Several of the incorrect answers also focus more on the social worker's career and correct responses are always those that most directly relate to the delivery of effective client services. Social workers have to be careful not to get "into a rut," and must consider the unique circumstances of each client when assessing need and intervening.

Knowledge Area

Unit II—Assessment (Content Area); Assessment Methods and Techniques (Competency); Methods of Involving Clients/Client Systems in Problem Identification (e.g., Gathering Collateral Information) (KSA)

164. D

Rationale

The high prevalence of **comorbidity between Substance Use Disorders and mental illnesses** does not mean that one causes the other, even if one appears first. In fact, establishing causality or directionality is difficult for several reasons. Diagnosis of a mental disorder may not occur until symptoms have progressed to a specified level (per *DSM-5*); however, subclinical symptoms may also prompt drug use, and imperfect recollections of when drug use started can create confusion as to which came first.

One hypothesis is that drug abuse can cause abusers to experience one or more behavioral health symptoms that may appear to be a mental illness. Thus, drug abuse may seem to cause mental disorders. A second hypothesis is that both Substance Use Disorders and mental illnesses are caused by overlapping factors such as underlying brain deficits, genetic vulnerabilities, and/or early exposure to stress or trauma.

A third hypothesis, based on the concept of self-medication, is that mental illnesses can lead to drug abuse. Individuals with overt, mild, or even subclinical mental disorders may abuse drugs as a form of self-medication. For example, the use of tobacco products by those with Schizophrenia is believed to lessen the symptoms of the disease and improve cognition.

Test-Taking Strategies Applied

The question contains a qualifying word—BEST. Although some of the incorrect response choices are true, they do not support the notion of self-medication or taking drugs, illicitly or otherwise, to treat a problem without medical advice. There may be a propensity to take drugs for the purpose of lessening mental health symptoms that support the notion of self-medication.

Knowledge Area

Unit II—Assessment (Content Area); Assessment Methods and Techniques (Competency); Co-Occurring Disorders and Conditions (KSA)

165. A

Rationale

Social workers often use **collateral sources**—family, friends, other agencies, physicians, and so on—as informants when collecting information to effectively treat clients. These sources can provide vital information when other professionals or agencies may have treated clients in the past. Family members and friends may also provide important information about the length or severity of issues or problems.

Collateral information is often used when the credibility and validity of information obtained from a client or others are questionable. When an account by a collateral informant agrees with information gathered from a client, it enhances the trustworthiness of the data collected. Using multiple information sources (or triangulation) is an excellent method for social workers to have accurate accounts upon which to make assessments or base interventions.

It is essential that a social worker get a client's informed consent prior to reaching out to collateral sources.

Test-Taking Strategies Applied

The question contains a qualifying word—TRUE. It is even capitalized to assist with identifying the distinguishing factor of the correct response from the rest. Each statement must be read carefully and evaluated as to its accuracy. The correct answer is identified through the process of elimination, with each false assertion being excluded.

The standards about informed consent in the *NASW Code of Ethics* should be recalled when evaluating the validity of each response choice.

Knowledge Area

Unit II—Assessment (Content Area); Assessment Methods and Techniques (Competency); Methods of Involving Clients/Client Systems in Problem Identification (e.g., Gathering Collateral Information) (KSA)

166. B

Rationale

Utilization review is the process of making sure services are being used appropriately. The goal of utilization review is to make sure clients get the care they need and that it is administered via proven methods, provided by an appropriate provider, and delivered in an appropriate setting. Utilization review is very frequently done in health care settings. Utilization review can be done while the care is being given, known as a concurrent review, or after the care has been completed, known as a retrospective review. It aims to ensure that high-quality care is delivered effectively and efficiently.

Capitation is a payment arrangement that pays providers a set amount for each client assigned to them, per period of time, whether or not that client seeks care. It pays per client rather than per service, with the incentive of controlling costs through the elimination of unnecessary services being delivered.

Level of care is the intensity of services provided.

Peer grouping in health care aims to group providers by defined characteristics (size, type of care, and so on).

Test-Taking Strategies Applied

This is a recall question that relies on social workers understanding terms related to the service delivery, especially those in health care. Although all of the terms may relate to cost and/or care, only one is concerned with both simultaneously. The word "monitor" is also important as utilization review is an *ongoing* activity that uses information to make individual client decisions as well as system improvements.

Knowledge Area

Unit III—Interventions With Clients/Client Systems (Content Area); Intervention Processes and Techniques (Competency); Techniques Used to Evaluate a Client's/Client System's Progress (KSA)

167. B

Rationale

Sexual activity of adults is integral to physical and mental health.

Older adults who are having sex with people other than life partners have to worry about sexually transmitted diseases (STDs) just as much as younger adults in the same situation, and they should be practicing safer sex by using condoms.

Older women and men experience physical changes that can lead to difficulties in sexual activity. However, the aging process does not have to result in sexual dissatisfaction. In fact, many older adults have very rewarding sex lives.

Vaginal walls become thinner as women age, and vaginal intercourse may be painful for women because there is less vaginal lubrication and the entrance to the vagina becomes smaller. Male erections may occur more slowly once testosterone production slows. Men also become less able to have another erection after an orgasm and may take up to 24 hours to achieve and sustain another erection.

Most older adults are interested in sex, and many lead active sex lives and enjoy sexual activity. Although adult men and women go through some sexual changes as they age, they do not lose their desire or their ability for sexual expression. Even for those who are very old, the need for touch and intimacy remains, although the desire and ability to have sexual intercourse may lessen.

Test-Taking Strategies Applied

The question contains a qualifying word—TRUE. It is even capitalized to assist with identifying the distinguishing factor of the correct response from the rest. Each statement must be read carefully and evaluated as to its accuracy. The correct answer is identified through the process of elimination, with each false assertion being excluded.

Knowledge Area

Unit I—Human Development, Diversity, and Behavior in the Environment (Content Area); Human Growth and Development (Competency); Theories of Sexual Development Throughout the Lifespan (KSA)

168. A

Rationale

Social workers respect and promote the right of clients to **self-determination**. The right to self-determination must be respected even when social workers feel that clients are making poor choices.

Test-Taking Strategies Applied

The question assesses social workers' ethical mandate to respect clients' decisions even if they are thought to be faulty. The other three answers may be actions that a social worker would like to or would take given the specifics in the case scenario. However, the correct answer gets at the root of the KSA being assessed—protecting and enhancing client system self-determination. The social worker must acknowledge that right, regardless of any other actions taken. In all instances, social workers should not be judgmental about clients' decisions, respecting their actions and decisions unless they pose serious, foreseeable, and imminent risk to themselves or others.

Knowledge Area

Unit IV—Professional Relationships, Values, and Ethics (Content Area); Professional Values and Ethical Issues (Competency); Client/Client System Competence and Self-Determination (e.g., Financial Decisions, Treatment Decisions, Emancipation, Age of Consent, Permanency Planning) (KSA)

169. B

Rationale

The goal of **supervision** is used to train and support social workers so that they can *provide clients with the most effective and efficient services possible*. Supervision provides social workers with the structure and agency resources that enable them to do their jobs effectively (administrative supervision); increases social workers' knowledge and skills and ability to do their jobs effectively (educational supervision); and sustains social workers emotionally in the performance of their jobs (supportive supervision). These primary functions of supervision— administrative, educational, and supportive—overlap and are interrelated.

   Evaluation is incorporated into all three domains as supervisors need to determine resources needed, knowledge gaps, and/or support needs. However, evaluation itself is not one of the primary functions of supervision.

Test-Taking Strategies Applied

The question contains a qualifying word—NOT—that requires social workers to select the response choice that is not one of the primary functions of supervision. Primary is also a qualifying word, though it is not capitalized. Although evaluation is critical to each of the three functions, it is too specific to be considered a primary purpose by itself.

Knowledge Area

Unit IV—Professional Relationships, Values, and Ethics (Content Area); Professional Development and Use of Self (Competency); Models of Supervision and Consultation (e.g., Individual, Peer, Group) (KSA)

170. D

Rationale

Political action is an ethical responsibility of social workers to the broader society. According to the *NASW Code of Ethics*, social workers should engage in social and political action that seeks to ensure that all people have equal access to the resources, employment, services, and opportunities they require to meet their basic human needs and to develop fully. Social workers should be aware of the impact of the political arena on practice and should advocate for changes in policy and legislation to improve social conditions in order to meet basic human needs and promote social justice.

Test-Taking Strategies Applied

The question contains a qualifying word—BEST. Although some of the response choices may be partially true or are valid, only one most aptly describes the ethical mandate of social workers as per the *NASW Code of Ethics*. Whenever ethical mandates of social workers are the foci of questions, the *NASW Code of Ethics* must be recalled. The answer that most closely resembles the wording of the *NASW Code of Ethics* should be selected. Although political action may be prohibited by social workers employed in the executive branch of government, this is a job restriction, not an ethical mandate as per the *NASW Code of Ethics*. This question is asking about social workers' ethical responsibilities to broader society.

Knowledge Area

Unit I—Human Development, Diversity, and Behavior in the Environment (Content Area); Diversity, Social/Economic Justice, and Oppression (Competency); The Impact of the Political Environment on Policy-Making (KSA)

Evaluation of Results

These tables assist in identifying the content areas and competencies needing further study. Within each of the competencies, there are specific Knowledge, Skills, and Abilities (KSAs) that social workers should reference to assist with locating appropriate study resources. As there is tremendous overlap in the material that could be contained across the KSAs within a given competency, all KSAs for the competency should be reviewed to make sure of an adequate breadth of knowledge in the content area. A listing of the KSAs for each content area and competency can be found in Appendix A.

The results of this evaluation should be the basis of the development of a study plan. Social workers should get to a level of comfort with the material so that they can summarize relevant content, including key concepts and terms. Social workers do not need to be experts in all of the KSAs, but should understand their relevancy to social work practice. They should be able to describe how each of the KSAs specifically impacts assessment, as well as decisions about client care.

Appendix B provides useful information on learning styles that can assist when determining the best ways to study and retain material. Success on the Association of Social Word Boards (ASWB®) examination does not require a lot of memorization of material, but rather the ability to recall terms and integrate multiple concepts to select the best course of action in hypothetical scenarios. Thus, time is best spent really understanding the KSAs and not just being able to recite definitions.

Analysis of Bachelors Practice Test

Unit I: Human Development, Diversity, and Behavior in the Environment (25%)

Competency	Question Numbers	Number of Questions	Number Correct	Percentage Correct	Area Requiring Further Study?
1. Human Growth and Development	1, 3, 4, 26, 30, 39, 41, 103, 104, 105, 125, 133, 157, 167	14	___/14	___%	
2. Human Behavior in the Social Environment	6, 27, 45, 53, 54, 57, 70, 71, 93, 141, 148, 159	12	___/12	___%	
3. Diversity, Social/ Economic Justice, and Oppression	11, 18, 31, 44, 55, 66, 72, 78, 89, 100, 102, 110, 121, 138, 139, 154, 170	17	___/17	___%	

Competency	Question Numbers	Number of Questions	Number Correct	Percentage Correct	Area Requiring Further Study?
Analysis of Bachelors Practice Test Unit II: Assessment (29%)					
4. Biopsychosocial History and Collateral Data	10, 50, 52, 91, 92, 118, 122, 126, 151, 155	10	___/10	___%	
5. Assessment Methods and Techniques	17, 23, 28, 34, 36, 40, 48, 62, 63, 73, 79, 80, 81, 82, 84, 85, 87, 98, 99, 106, 107, 129, 134, 135, 136, 142, 143, 144, 147, 156, 162, 163, 164, 165	34	___/34	___%	
6. Concepts of Abuse and Neglect	46, 49, 77, 131, 161	5	___/5	___%	

Analysis of Bachelors Practice Test
Unit III: Interventions With Clients/Client Systems (26%)

Competency	Question Numbers	Number of Questions	Number Correct	Percentage Correct	Area Requiring Further Study?
7. Indicators and Effects of Crisis and Change	37, 61, 95, 97, 109, 146	6	___/6	___%	
8. Intervention Processes and Techniques	2, 5, 9, 16, 20, 22, 35, 38, 47, 58, 59, 64, 65, 68, 74, 83, 86, 88, 96, 108, 111, 114, 115, 116, 127, 128, 152, 153, 166	29	___/29	___%	
9. Use of Collaborative Relationships	21, 29, 51, 94, 113, 119, 145	7	___/7	___%	
10. Documentation	60, 117	2	___/2	___%	

Analysis of Bachelors Practice Test
Unit IV: Professional Relationships, Values, and Ethics (20%)

Competency	Question Numbers	Number of Questions	Number Correct	Percentage Correct	Area Requiring Further Study?
11. Professional Values and Ethical Issues	12, 13, 15, 24, 25, 42, 43, 90, 120, 123, 130, 140, 158, 168	14	___/14	___%	
12. Confidentiality	14, 19, 33, 67, 69, 112, 137, 149, 150	9	___/9	___%	
13. Professional Development and Use of Self	7, 8, 32, 56, 75, 76, 101, 124, 132, 160, 169	11	___/11	___%	

Overall Results of Bachelors Practice Test				
	Content Area	Number of Questions	Number Correct	Percentage Correct
Unit I (25%)	Human Development, Diversity, and Behavior in the Environment	43	___/43	___%
Unit II (29%)	Assessment	49	___/49	___%
Unit III (26%)	Interventions With Clients/ Client Systems	44	___/44	___%
Unit IV (20%)	Professional Relationships, Values, and Ethics	34	___/34	___%
Overall Knowledge	ASWB® Bachelors Examination	170	___/170	___%

Appendix A

Content Areas, Competencies, and KSAs for the ASWB® Bachelors Examination

Human Development, Diversity, and Behavior in the Environment (Content Area)

1. Human Growth and Development (Competency)

KSAs
Theories of human development throughout the lifespan (e.g., physical, social, emotional, cognitive, behavioral)
The indicators of normal and abnormal physical, cognitive, emotional, and sexual development throughout the lifespan
Theories of sexual development throughout the lifespan
Theories of spiritual development throughout the lifespan
Theories of racial, ethnic, and cultural development throughout the lifespan
The effects of physical, mental, and cognitive disabilities throughout the lifespan
The interplay of biological, psychological, social, and spiritual factors
Basic human needs
The principles of attachment and bonding
The effect of aging on biopsychosocial functioning
The impact of aging parents on adult children

Gerontology

Personality theories

Theories of conflict

Factors influencing self-image (e.g., culture, race, religion/spirituality, age, disability, trauma)

Body image and its impact (e.g., identity, self-esteem, relationships, habits)

Parenting skills and capacities

2. Human Behavior in the Social Environment (Competency)

KSAs

The family life cycle

Family dynamics and functioning and the effects on individuals, families, groups, organizations, and communities

Theories of couples development

The impact of physical and mental illness on family dynamics

Psychological defense mechanisms and their effects on behavior and relationships

Addiction theories and concepts

Systems and ecological perspectives and theories

Role theories

Theories of group development and functioning

Theories of social change and community development

The dynamics of interpersonal relationships

Models of family life education in social work practice

Strengths-based and resilience theories

3. Diversity, Social/Economic Justice, and Oppression (Competency)

KSAs

Feminist theory

The effect of disability on biopsychosocial functioning throughout the lifespan

The effect of culture, race, and ethnicity on behaviors, attitudes, and identity

The effects of discrimination and stereotypes on behaviors, attitudes, and identity

The influence of sexual orientation on behaviors, attitudes, and identity

The impact of transgender and transitioning process on behaviors, attitudes, identity, and relationships

Systemic (institutionalized) discrimination (e.g., racism, sexism, ageism)

The principles of culturally competent social work practice

Sexual orientation concepts
Gender and gender identity concepts
The impact of social institutions on society
The effect of poverty on individuals, families, groups, organizations, and
    communities
The impact of the environment (e.g., social, physical, cultural, political,
    economic) on individuals, families, groups, organizations, and
    communities
Person-in-environment (PIE) theory
Social and economic justice
Criminal justice systems
The effects of life events, stressors, and crises on individuals, families,
    groups, organizations, and communities
The impact of the political environment on policy-making

Assessment (Content Area)

4. Biopsychosocial History and Collateral Data (Competency)

KSAs
The components of a biopsychosocial assessment
The components and function of the mental status examination
Biopsychosocial responses to illness and disability
Biopsychosocial factors related to mental health
The indicators of psychosocial stress
Basic medical terminology
The indicators of mental and emotional illness throughout the lifespan
The types of information available from other sources (e.g., agency,
    employment, medical, psychological, legal, or school records)

5. Assessment Methods and Techniques (Competency)

KSAs
The factors and processes used in problem formulation
Methods of involving clients/client systems in problem identification
    (e.g., gathering collateral information)
Techniques and instruments used to assess clients/client systems
Methods to incorporate the results of psychological and educational tests
    into assessment
Communication theories and styles
The concept of congruence in communication
Risk assessment methods

Methods to assess the client's/client system's strengths, resources, and
    challenges (e.g., individual, family, group, organization, community)
The indicators of motivation, resistance, and readiness to change
Methods to assess motivation, resistance, and readiness to change
Methods to assess the client's/client system's communication skills
Methods to assess the client's/client system's coping abilities
The indicators of the client's/client system's strengths and challenges
Methods used to assess trauma
Placement options based on assessed level of care
The effects of addiction and substance abuse on individuals, families,
    groups, organizations, and communities
The indicators of addiction and substance abuse
Co-occurring disorders and conditions
The Diagnostic and Statistical Manual of the American Psychiatric
    Association
The indicators of behavioral dysfunction
The indicators of somatization
The indicators of feigning illness
Common psychotropic and non-psychotropic prescriptions and over-the-
    counter medications and their side effects

6. Concepts of Abuse and Neglect (Competency)

KSAs
Indicators and dynamics of abuse and neglect throughout the lifespan
The effects of physical, sexual, and psychological abuse on individuals,
    families, groups, organizations, and communities
The indicators, dynamics, and impact of exploitation across the lifespan
    (e.g., financial, immigration status, sexual trafficking)
The characteristics of perpetrators of abuse, neglect, and exploitation

Interventions With Clients/Client Systems (Content Area)

7. Indicators and Effects of Crisis and Change (Competency)

KSAs
The impact of out-of-home placement (e.g., hospitalization, foster care,
    residential care, criminal justice system) on clients/client systems
The impact of stress, trauma, and violence
Theories of trauma-informed care
Crisis intervention theories
The indicators of traumatic stress and violence

The impact of out-of-home displacement (e.g., natural disaster, homelessness, immigration) on clients/client systems

The indicators and risk factors of the client's/client system's danger to self and others

Methods and approaches to trauma-informed care

The impact of caregiving on families

The dynamics and effects of loss, separation, and grief

8. Intervention Processes and Techniques (Competency)

KSAs

The principles and techniques of interviewing (e.g., supporting, clarifying, focusing, confronting, validating, feedback, reflecting, language differences, use of interpreters, redirecting)

Methods to involve clients/client systems in intervention planning

Cultural considerations in the creation of an intervention plan

The criteria used in the selection of intervention/treatment modalities (e.g., client/client system abilities, culture, life stage)

The components of intervention, treatment, and service plans

Psychotherapies

The impact of immigration, refugee, or undocumented status on service delivery

Discharge, aftercare, and follow-up planning

The phases of intervention and treatment

The principles and techniques for building and maintaining a helping relationship

The client's/client system's role in the problem-solving process

Problem-solving models and approaches (e.g., brief, solution-focused methods or techniques)

Methods to engage and motivate clients/client systems

Methods to engage and work with involuntary clients/client systems

Methods to obtain and provide feedback

The principles of active listening and observation

Verbal and nonverbal communication techniques

Limit setting techniques

The technique of role play

Role modeling techniques

Methods to obtain sensitive information (e.g., substance abuse, sexual abuse)

Techniques for harm reduction for self and others

Methods to teach coping and other self-care skills to clients/client systems

Client/client system self-monitoring techniques

Methods to develop, review, and implement crisis plans

Methods of conflict resolution

Crisis intervention and treatment approaches

Anger management techniques

Stress management techniques

Cognitive and behavioral interventions

Strengths-based and empowerment strategies and interventions

Client/client system contracting and goal-setting techniques

Partializing techniques

Assertiveness training

Task-centered approaches

Psychoeducation methods (e.g., acknowledging, supporting, normalizing)

Group work techniques and approaches (e.g., developing and managing group processes and cohesion)

Family therapy models, interventions, and approaches

Permanency planning

Mindfulness and complementary therapeutic approaches

The components of case management

Techniques used for follow-up

The elements of a case presentation

Methods of service delivery

Concepts of social policy development and analysis

Theories and methods of advocacy for policies, services, and resources to meet clients'/client systems' needs

Community organizing and social planning methods

Techniques for mobilizing community participation

Methods to develop and evaluate measurable objectives for client/client system intervention, treatment, and/or service plans

Techniques used to evaluate a client's/client system's progress

Primary, secondary, and tertiary prevention strategies

Methods to create, implement, and evaluate policies and procedures that minimize risk for individuals, families, groups, organizations, and communities

The impact of domestic, intimate partner, and other violence on the helping relationship

The indicators of client/client system readiness for termination

Methods, techniques, and instruments used to evaluate social work practice

Evidence-based practice

9. Use of Collaborative Relationships (Competency)

KSAs

The basic terminology of professions other than social work (e.g., legal, educational)

The effect of the client's developmental level on the social worker–client relationship

Methods to clarify the roles and responsibilities of the social worker and client/client system in the intervention process

Consultation approaches (e.g., referrals to specialists)

Methods of networking

The process of interdisciplinary and intradisciplinary team collaboration

Methods to assess the availability of community resources

Methods to establish service networks or community resources

The effects of policies, procedures, regulations, and legislation on social work practice and service delivery

The relationship between formal and informal power structures in the decision-making process

10. Documentation (Competency)

KSAs

The principles of case recording, documentation, and management of practice records

The elements of client/client system reports

The principles and processes for developing formal documents (e.g., proposals, letters, brochures, pamphlets, reports, evaluations)

The principles and features of objective and subjective data

Professional Relationships, Values, and Ethics (Content Area)

11. Professional Values and Ethical Issues (Competency)

KSAs

Legal and/or ethical issues related to the practice of social work, including responsibility to clients/client systems, colleagues, the profession, and society

Professional values and principles (e.g., competence, social justice, integrity, and dignity and worth of the person)

The influence of the social worker's own values and beliefs on the social worker–client/client system relationship

The dynamics of diversity in the social worker–client/client system relationship

Techniques to identify and resolve ethical dilemmas

Client/client system competence and self-determination (e.g., financial decisions, treatment decisions, emancipation, age of consent, permanency planning)

Techniques for protecting and enhancing client/client system self-determination

The client's/client system's right to refuse services (e.g., medication, medical treatment, counseling, placement, etc.)

The dynamics of power and transparency in the social worker–client/client system relationship

Professional boundaries in the social worker–client/client system relationship (e.g., power differences, conflicts of interest, etc.)

Ethical issues related to dual relationships

Legal and/or ethical issues regarding mandatory reporting (e.g., abuse, threat of harm, impaired professionals, etc.)

Legal and/or ethical issues regarding documentation

Legal and/or ethical issues regarding termination

Legal and/or ethical issues related to death and dying

Research ethics (e.g., institutional review boards, use of human subjects, informed consent)

Ethical issues in supervision and management

Methods to create, implement, and evaluate policies and procedures for social worker safety

12. Confidentiality (Competency)

KSAs

The principles and processes of obtaining informed consent

The use of client/client system records

Legal and/or ethical issues regarding confidentiality, including electronic information security

13. Professional Development and Use of Self (Competency)

KSAs

The components of the social worker–client/client system relationship

The social worker's role in the problem-solving process

The concept of acceptance and empathy in the social worker–client/client system relationship

The impact of transference and countertransference in the social worker–client/client system relationship

Social worker self-care principles and techniques

Burnout, secondary trauma, and compassion fatigue

The components of a safe and positive work environment

Professional objectivity in the social worker–client/client system relationship

Self-disclosure principles and applications

The influence of the social worker's own values and beliefs on interdisciplinary collaboration

Governance structures

Accreditation and/or licensing requirements

Time management approaches

Models of supervision and consultation (e.g., individual, peer, group)

The supervisee's role in supervision (e.g., identifying learning needs, self-assessment, prioritizing, etc.)

The impact of transference and countertransference within supervisory relationships

Professional development activities to improve practice and maintain current professional knowledge (e.g., in-service training, licensing requirements, reviews of literature, workshops)

Appendix B

Learning Styles

The following are some suggested techniques for each learning style that can help to fill in content gaps that may exist.

VISUAL LEARNERS

Visual learners learn best through what they see. Although lectures can be boring for visual learners, they benefit from the use of diagrams, PowerPoint slides, and charts.

- Use colored highlighters to draw attention to key terms
- Develop outlines or take notes on the concepts
- Write talking points for each of the Knowledge, Skills, and Abilities (KSAs) on separate white index cards
- Create a coding schema of symbols and write them next to material and terms that require further study
- Study in an environment that is away from visual distractions such as television, people moving around, or clutter

AUDITORY LEARNERS

Auditory learners learn best through what they hear. They may have difficulty remembering material, but can easily recall it if it is read to them.

- Tape-record yourself summarizing the material as you are studying it—listen to your notes as a way to reinforce what you read
- Have a study partner explain the relevant concepts and terms related to the KSAs
- Read the text aloud if you are having trouble remembering it
- Find free podcasts or YouTube videos on the Internet on the content areas that are short and easy to understand to assist with learning
- Talk to yourself about the content as you study, emphasizing what is important to remember related to each KSA

KINESTHETIC OR HANDS-ON LEARNERS

Kinesthetic learners learn through tactile approaches aimed at experiencing or doing. They need physical activities as a foundation for instruction.

- Make flashcards on material because writing it down will assist with remembering the content
- Use as many different senses as possible when studying—read material when you are on your treadmill, use highlighters, talk aloud about content, and/or listen to a study partner
- Develop mnemonic devices to aid in information retention (e.g., EAPIET or *EAt PIE T*oday is a great way to remember the social work problem-solving process [Engaging, Assessing, Planning, Intervening, Evaluating, and Terminating])
- Write notes and important terms in the margins
- Ask a study partner to quiz you on material—turn it into a game and see how many KSAs you can discuss or how long you can talk about a content area before running out of material